Praise for
Little Strength, Big God

"This book reminds us that the challenges we face are not unlike what people of character have faced for all of history. With thought-provoking examples, Debbie gently guides us in making decisions now regarding our integrity and faith for the situations we are likely to encounter along the way. No matter your circumstances or position today, you will create a shield of protection by reading this book."

—**Dan Miller,** author of *48 Days to the Work You Love*

"In our world of ever-increasing antagonism, Debbie Wilson shows how those in the Bible faced similar challenges and found strength in the Lord. Like these heroes of the faith, we can triumph in crushing circumstances. *Little Strength, Big God* provides assurance, hope, and practical steps."

—**PeggySue Wells,** best-selling author of 31 books, including *The Ten Best Decisions a Single Mom Can Make*, *Chasing Sunrise*, and *The Patent*

"I absolutely love Debbie Wilson's latest book and see it as a great gift for our world at this moment in history when it is hard to stand strong for what is real, true, and good. Debbie's personal anecdotes accompanying each topic are by far my favorite part of the book, bringing to life human stories of radical trust in God in a variety of situations and his ensuing fidelity to his children. I highly recommend *Little Strength, Big God* for anyone wanting to take their faith to the next level!"

—**Jeanne F. Mancini,** President, March for Life Action

"*Little Strength, Big God* is a powerful reminder of the mighty strength of our God. Just as he was bigger than all the problems faced by the people in Hebrews 11, he is bigger than all our trials, challenges, and mistakes. While current issues have different names, many of the problems remain the same. This book is a refreshing reminder to view our problems through a God lens and not vice versa. *Little Strength, Big God* will strengthen you and your faith."

—**Lisa T. Grimes,** author and cofounder of Habergeon and Lead Wholly

"Debbie Wilson's *Little Strength, Big God* does not disappoint. She's created a compelling study of God's faithfulness to his people through engaging (and sometimes little-known) Bible stories. The format provides a strong and comprehensive understanding of Scripture as Wilson blends ancient examples from the Bible with modern-day accounts. I recommend this book for serious students of God's Word and for those who long to go deeper. This is a book I will return to time and again."

—**Deb DeArmond,** award-winning author and writing coach

"Debbie Wilson has written an anointed book that overflows with the power of God the Father, God the Son, and God the Holy Spirit. With her own stories and those of others, she shows us how we can stand in God's strength for what is right. The most freeing statement came when Wilson wrote about David facing the Goliaths (giants) in his life in God's strength, but *as David*. As a believer, I will face the giants in my life *as Yvonne*, 'not as a soldier in someone else's armor.' Each of us has that privilege and blessing. I highly recommend this book for all who call themselves believers and for those who are searching for something worth believing."

—**Yvonne Ortega,** international speaker, author of the Moving from Broken to Beautiful series, recently retired Licensed Professional Counselor, AWSA Coach

"The world tells us, 'You can do it! Get brave and overcome.' We do our best to fight the good fight of faith, but when we fall short in our strength, we feel like failures. In *Little Strength, Big God*, Debbie W. Wilson shows us how those we call heroes of faith found their strength when they didn't think they had what it took to step into God's calling. This book is an excellent reminder that we don't have to have it all together. When our strength is little or we feel we don't have any strength, our God is faithful to give us his strength in the battle and for daily living."

—**Patty Mason,** best-selling author of *Getting to Know God's Heart*

"Has God called you into the overwhelming? Are you intimidated as you face the seemingly impossible? In *Little Strength, Big God*, Debbie Wilson finds insightful and inspiring wisdom from Old Testament stories for facing our giants. Digging deep into the Word, she offers beautiful glimpses of the unfailing faithfulness of God. If you are seeking realistic expectations of God in the twenty-first century and want to find your strength in his power and ability, this book was written for you. Refresh your faith in the God of the impossible and read it!"

—**Julie Zine Coleman,** author of *On Purpose*, and managing editor of the AriseDaily devotional website

"*Little Strength, Big God* is one of the best Bible studies I've ever done. It will help grow your trust in the immeasurable power of God, who is especially close to all who call on him—particularly the imperfect, those who feel weak or insecure, and those riddled with fear. This book will be at the top of my list of recommended studies!"

—**Tara Furman,** Founder and President of Knowing God Ministries

"Debbie W. Wilson's vivid imagery seamlessly weaves biblical truth with the struggles of real people through the ages. *Little Strength, Big God* will take you by the hand and show you how your weakness is your greatest strength, plaings your hand in God's."

—**Rhonda Robinson,** award-winning author of *FreeFall: Holding onto Faith When the Unthinkable Strikes*

Little Strength Big God

for
Christopher & Chelsea,

Much love,

Debbie

Heb. 11:6

Little Strength Big God

Discover a God Greater than Your Goliaths

Debbie W. Wilson

LEAFWOOD
PUBLISHERS

an imprint of Abilene Christian University Press

LITTLE STRENGTH, BIG GOD
Discover a God Greater than Your Goliaths

LEAFWOOD
PUBLISHERS
an imprint of Abilene Christian University Press

Copyright © 2023 by Debbie W. Wilson

ISBN 978-1-68426-352-3

Printed in the United States of America

Scripture quotations, unless otherwise noted, are from The Holy Bible, New International Version®, NIV®. Copyright © 1973, 1978, 1984, 2011 by Biblica, Inc.® Used by permission. All rights reserved worldwide.

Scripture quotations noted NASB are taken from the New American Standard Bible® Copyright © 1960, 1962, 1963, 1968, 1971, 1972, 1973, 1975, 1977, 1995 by The Lockman Foundation. Used by permission.

Scripture quotations noted NLT are taken from the Holy Bible, New Living Translation, copyright ©1996, 2004, 2007 by Tyndale House Foundation. Used by permission of Tyndale House Publishers, Inc., Carol Stream, IL 60188. All rights reserved.

Scripture quotations noted GW are taken from GOD'S WORD®. © 1995, 2003, 2013, 2014, 2019, 2020 by God's Word to the Nations Mission Society. Used by permission.

Published in association with PeggySue Wells, Write Way 3419 E 1000, North Roanoke, IN 46783.

Cataloging-in-Publication Data is on file at the Library of Congress, Washington, DC.

Cover design by Thinkpen Design, LLC | Interior text design by Sandy Armstrong, Strong Design

Leafwood Publishers is an imprint of Abilene Christian University Press
ACU Box 29138
Abilene, Texas 79699

1-877-816-4455
www.leafwoodpublishers.com

23 24 25 26 27 28 29 / 7 6 5 4 3 2 1

To Susie, I kept my promise.

To Lisa, a tower of strength and a steadfast friend.

To Diane, a living example of Philippians 4:13.

Contents

Foreword

I WAS TIRED AND SUSCEPTIBLE TO THE VOICE OF DISCOUR-
agement. Someone had hurt my feelings with wounding words and
actions. So now, as I worked on my latest project, I could hear the
whispers of the enemy, "Why are you wasting your life? Just quit."

Quit? I love the Lord with all my heart, and I will follow him
wherever he leads me, even when it means standing up to harsh
words or working on thankless tasks.

When the enemy assaults me, I push forward, not in my
strength but in God's. I push past the voice of darkness as it whispers, "Give up already."

We've all heard this whisper to surrender in our times of grief,
pain, and difficulties—a whisper that comes with a choice. We can
agree with the enemy's lies, or we can call for God's help so we can
push toward a breakthrough.

The apostle Paul encouraged us in 1 Corinthians 15:58: "Therefore,
my dear brothers and sisters, stand firm. Let nothing move you.
Always give yourselves fully to the work of the Lord, because you
know that your labor in the Lord is not in vain."

Paul's words remind us we need to call for the strength of the
Lord to empower us. Our own frail strength is not enough.

That's what I love about Debbie W. Wilson's latest book, *Little Strength, Big God*. It will help you find God's strength, empowering you to fulfill your purpose and face your battles with quiet confidence and courage.

Linda Evans Shepherd

Best-Selling Author and Founder of the Advanced Writers and Speakers Association

How to Get the Most Out of this Book

"GINNY, THE COMPANY'S TARGETED YOU," MY DAUGHTER'S supervisor said.

My daughter had excelled in her job with an international company for many years. Her performance repeatedly ranked in the top 5 percent worldwide. Suddenly, headquarters filed numerous complaints against this high performer.

No one could tell her what she needed to change because the complaints were not based on work performance. Despite successfully refuting these allegations, the false charges continued. Based on programs the company promotes, her conservative social media posts put her in their crosshairs.

How do we live and thrive in an antagonistic environment? For Christians, this has become an increasingly relevant concern. But the situation is not new to God's people. The men and women featured in the last half of Hebrews 11 lived in extremely hostile times. Many lived and worked under oppressive rulers. Each demonstrated an aspect of finding strength in the Lord that allowed them to triumph in crushing circumstances.

A good English teacher shows her students how to use nouns and verbs to build sentences and paragraphs to convey thoughts. Practicing these skills makes a student a better communicator. Similarly, the Lord provides the tools we need to become strong in battle. And while he fights for us, most battles require our participation. As we follow his lead, like those in Hebrews 11, we become "powerful in battle." Finding strength in the Lord removes the fear of people and circumstances and allows us to soar in situations that paralyze others.

The Layout

When I began writing *Little Faith, Big God*, I soon realized I needed two books to cover the men and women listed in Hebrews 11. In deciding how to divide them, the phrase "whose weakness was turned to strength; and who became powerful in battle" (v. 34) stood out to me. I felt it described the men and women in Hebrews 11:23–40 very well. This book explores those men and women and what we can learn from them.

The chapters in *Little Strength, Big God* are divided into five daily lessons to be studied at the speed that suits you or your group. Each chapter begins with a vignette of a biblical character's life, as I imagine it. Each day includes an introduction, followed by a Study and Reflection section with questions to guide the personal application of Scripture. The day concludes with a Strength Builder and a place for you to record a closing prayer. Day Five ends with a place to record prayer requests for those meeting with a group.

This study is written to help you become a biblical thinker and an able listener of God. Use a Bible in a translation you enjoy. Below are a few suggestions to help optimize your experience:

- Bring a pen.
- Feel free to add your own questions.

- Listening to passages read aloud helps me hear things I miss when silently reading the same passage. Consider listening to the biblical stories in a familiar version or a modern idiomatic translation like *The Message*. There are several free audio Bible apps available.
- Since the Bible is spiritually discerned (1 Cor. 2:9–16), begin each lesson by opening your heart and asking the Lord to speak to you through the Holy Spirit.
- Be open with the Lord and yourself when answering the questions. If you discuss this study with a group or another person, share only what you are comfortable sharing.
- When possible, do this study with a grace-filled group that enjoys discussion. We can learn much from other people's questions and observations.

May this study inspire and equip you to live strong and finish well.

Lord Jesus, thank you for inviting us to live every day with you. Grant us ears to hear, eyes to see, and hearts to receive all you have for us. In Jesus's name. Amen.

*Note for those planning group studies, you can find a leader's guide at debbiewwilson.com/book. Allow eight weeks for discussion if you plan to cover one chapter per week. However, some weeks can be divided into smaller chunks for deeper discussion. For example, because there's more biblical reading on Moses in Week Two, you could divide that discussion into two weeks. In Week Seven, you could discuss Days 1–3 one week and Days 4 and 5 the following. In Week Eight, you could discuss David in one session and spiritual armor in another the following week. Depending on how you split these weeks, your study could run from eight to eleven weeks.

If your group has only a brief time to cover the lesson, ask the group to come prepared to share one or two takeaways from each day. When the group meets, the facilitator can summarize the main point for each day and ask the group members to share their takeaways from that day's lesson.

Strength to Resist Intimidation

Fear of man paralyzes; fear of God mobilizes.

"Oh, Amram, he's beautiful." Jochebed stroked their newborn's soft cheek.

Her husband nodded and squeezed her arm.

She met his eyes. "We must protect him."

"Yes, but how?" Amram threw up his hands. "What can two slaves do against Pharaoh and all of Egypt?"

Jochebed brushed away a tear. "We'll ask Yahweh to make a way."

"Eventually, a new king came to power in Egypt who knew nothing about Joseph or what he had done."
—Exodus 1:8 (NLT)

Exodus begins like a thriller. To forget Joseph meant to forget the debt Egypt owed his people. Joseph's wise leadership and God-given ability to interpret dreams had saved Egypt from total devastation hundreds of years earlier during a great famine. The grateful pharaoh of that time gave the land of Goshen to Joseph's family of shepherds. This new ruler disregarded Egypt's history and debt to Joseph and Joseph's God.

Like Hitler, Saddam Hussein, and the Taliban, this pharaoh ruled with an iron fist. Approximately 1500 years before Christ, Amram and Jochebed started their family under his oppressive reign. When harsh treatment failed to slow the growth of the Hebrew population, he commanded the Hebrew midwives to kill the baby boys as they were born. When that didn't work, he ordered all of Egypt to throw the male Hebrew babies into the Nile.

With no sonograms to predict the gender of a child and allow the family to brace themselves for what might follow, can you imagine the emotions that accompanied every Hebrew birth?

"It's a girl!" Exhales. Smiles. Embraces.

"It's a boy." Hands cover faces. Sobs.

These mothers loved their babies. These fathers needed to protect their families. But how could a slave resist the power of Egypt?

In this dark setting, five brave women dared to defy a cruel dictator and his people.

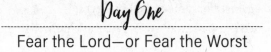

Day One

Fear the Lord—or Fear the Worst

"Fearing people is a dangerous trap,
but trusting the LORD means safety."
—Proverbs 29:25 (NLT)

Are you or someone you love embroiled in a massive struggle? Are you battling to save your health, marriage, child, or culture? The enemy is fearsome. Why did God choose you for this battle?

I've learned God chooses the weak. Weakness may be your greatest qualification. God's glory shines through the cracks we call limitations (2 Cor. 4:7). But he doesn't leave us in a fragile state. Describing some of God's heroes, Hebrews 11:34 says, "[Their] weakness was turned to strength." As Moses's parents and the two

Hebrew midwives illustrate, our limitations become windows through which God's glory shines.

Shiphrah and Puah cherished their jobs as midwives. While other Hebrew slaves labored under ruthless taskmasters, they welcomed new babies into the world. Amid the desperate suffering of their people, Shiphrah and Puah thanked God for this joy and the promise held within each new life.

One day, Pharaoh summoned the midwives. He ordered them to kill the baby boys as they were being born. Shiphrah and Puah never imagined anyone—even one as cold as Pharaoh—would demand something so heinous.

His orders soured their stomachs. They couldn't do it—wouldn't do it. But did they have a choice? Shiphrah and Puah shuddered to imagine what would happen if they disobeyed. If Pharaoh killed infants without a qualm, what would he do to two disobedient slaves?

On the other hand, though compelled by their ruler, what would happen to their souls if they complied? Yahweh's presence swathed every birth. How could they offend him? Hadn't he said, "Whoever sheds human blood, by humans shall their blood be shed; for in the image of God has God made mankind" (Gen. 9:6)? His sweet favor meant more than life.

Pharaoh wielded power, but, despite the Egyptians' beliefs, he was no god.

Recalling the Lord's character reminded them of their calling to protect life. Knowing what they couldn't do clarified what they must do. They would serve Yahweh whether he saved them or not. They would disobey Pharaoh and rescue as many infant boys as possible. And when—not if—Pharaoh called them to give an account of their actions, may Yahweh have mercy on them.

The dreaded day arrived. Shiphrah and Puah prayed to the one they served for strength as they answered Pharaoh's summons.

Scripture Reading..

EXODUS 1:8–21

ACTS 5:29

Study and Reflection

1. "Eventually, a new king came to power in Egypt who knew
    nothing about Joseph or what he had done" (Exod. 1:8 NLT).
    Egypt owed Joseph, Abraham's great-grandson, a great
    debt. Joseph's wisdom and leadership kept Egypt from utter
    desolation during a seven-year famine. Pharaoh's igno-
    rance of history brought Egypt and the Hebrews great pain.
    From Exodus 1:11–14, list the words that describe how the
    Egyptians treated the Hebrews.

2. Consider what it must have been like for the Hebrews to live
    and labor under Pharaoh. From where did the midwives find
    the strength to resist Pharaoh (Exod. 1:17)?

3. How did God show his approval of Shiprah and Puah
    (Exod. 1:20–21)?

4. Imagine a situation where your boss's command violates your
    conscience or God's principles. How can you apply the mid-
    wives' story to such a challenge?

5. How do you know when to resist authority (Acts 5:29)?

6. Record any final thoughts or takeaways from today's lesson.

Destructive Fear versus Saving Reverence

Getting Republicans and Democrats to agree on something is about as easy as going off sugar during Christmas. Yet, according to Dan Heath, in his book *Upstream*, the two groups are more alike than you might think.

In a speech, Heath explained the results of a poll conducted in Charlotte, North Carolina, with Black women who identified themselves as Democrats and White women who identified as Republicans. While the political pundits want us to believe we are worlds apart in our healthcare needs and desires, the poll results from these two groups showed otherwise. Their answers showed a 1 percent difference in priorities. The pie charts were virtually identical. Healthcare is not a Democrat, Republican, or race issue. It's a human concern.

Satan wields fear to divide and manipulate people. To secure power, leaders like Pharaoh use race, religion, ideologies, and even masks and vaccines to pit groups against each other. Worst-case scenarios spun through Pharaoh's mind. "'Look,' he said to his people, 'the Israelites have become far too numerous for us. Come, we must deal shrewdly with them or they will become even more numerous and, if war breaks out, will join our enemies, fight against us and leave the country'" (Exod. 1:9–10). Ironically, the more Pharaoh oppressed the Hebrews, "the more they multiplied" (Exod. 1:12).

Someone described FEAR as False Evidence Appearing Real. Have you ever been manipulated by disturbing what-ifs? What if I can't pay my bills? What if my child gets involved in an unhealthy relationship? What if cancer returns? Our spiritual enemy plants dark scenarios in our minds hoping to control us with fear.

The late R. C. Sproul said you can't have courage without fear. You don't need courage if you aren't afraid. It's natural to *feel* fearful. But the faithful obey God anyway. In Revelation 21:8, God shuts the cowardly out of heaven, not the fearful.

Need Courage? Look Up

Where did Shiphrah and Puah, two female slaves, find the strength to defy a dictator the Egyptians called a god? They "feared God."

Perhaps standing in Pharaoh's throne room reminded them of another throne. Yahweh, not Pharaoh, determined their destinies.

God provides grace for real trials, not for imagined what-ifs. Rather than focus on what Pharaoh might do to them, the two women conquered the dread of their enemy through reverence for God.

The Bible says, "Fear of the Lord is the foundation of wisdom. Knowledge of the Holy One results in good judgment" (Prov. 9:10 NLT). The midwives' fear of God provided the wisdom and courage they needed to act in this tough spot. When Pharaoh summoned them, perhaps God reminded them of one of the Hebrew women who had given birth before they had arrived to attend the birth, and they relayed that story. Miraculously, Pharaoh sent them home unharmed. God rewarded Shiphrah and Puah with families of their own.

The Protection of Holy Awe

Have you ever been jarred awake from a dream where it feels like you're falling? When I visited Yosemite, I learned that for some who ignore a healthy fear of heights, that nightmare becomes a sickening reality. The fear of plummeting over the side warned me to stand away from the edge.

Similarly, I grew up near the coast. I learned the patterns and characteristics of the sea and avoided strong undercurrents and being afloat during storms. The more familiar I became with the ocean, the more I respected its power.

We might compare fear of God with a respect of the ocean. The better we know God, the greater our awe. A healthy fear of God saves us from the destructive fear of people, no matter how high their position.

A friend I'll call Zeke experienced that protection when his boss told him to manipulate the numbers on two sales representatives so the company wouldn't have to pay the bonuses they had earned. Zeke refused, and his boss fired him on the spot.

Ironically, or should we say providentially, a recruiter telephoned that night to ask if he would interview for a new job.

"How did you know I was available?"

"I didn't," the recruiter said. "I just know your qualifications."

Jesus told his disciples not to worry about how to defend themselves when they were arrested (Matt. 10:19). The Holy Spirit would give them what to say. Jesus hasn't changed. There is no need to live in dread. Those who fear the Lord have a counselor and comforter to guide them on earth and eternal glory awaiting them in heaven (2 Cor. 4:17; 2 Tim. 2:12).

Today's Strength Builder

What persistent fear do you face? What truth about God could help you counter this fear?

CLOSING PRAYER

Use this space to turn your insights and responses into prayers.

Day Two

Fear of God Overcomes Fear of Unjust Leaders

*"Sin whispers to the wicked, deep within their hearts.
They have no fear of God at all. In their blind conceit,
they cannot see how wicked they really are."*
—Psalm 36:1–2 (NLT)

I bet you've met people who, when given a little authority, think they're God. They remind me of a story about when God met a German shepherd, a Doberman, and a cat at the pearly gates. He asked each of them about their beliefs. The German shepherd said, "I believe in being loyal to my master."

"Good," said God. "Sit on my right side. Doberman, what do you believe in?"

"I believe in protecting my master."

"Ah, you may sit to my left." God turned to the cat. "And what do you believe?"

"I believe," replied the cat, "you're sitting in my seat."[1]

I've dealt with a few unreasonable people in my life, but never one with Pharaoh's reach. People suffer when leaders try to take God's seat.

In an article about a victim of China's one-child policy, a journalist wrote about a woman who managed to hide her pregnancy for eight months. When the government enforcers discovered she was pregnant with her second child, they abducted her and lethally injected her unborn baby. She delivered a stillborn while in custody.

Mei Fong, journalist and author of *One Child*, wrote about her conversation with a member of China's population police. His team surprised a woman at night who, because of her pregnancy with an out-of-plan baby, had hidden in a nearby village.

"We surrounded the house. We were very quiet, but I don't know, somehow she must have heard something . . . because she ran." She ran and ran, her large abdomen protruding, until she reached a pond. She continued until water touched her neck. Trapped, she tearfully pleaded for mercy. Two women officials waded in and took her away.[2]

When Pharaoh couldn't coerce the Hebrew midwives to do his dirty work, he played God. He turned *everyone* into his population police force and made them discard every male Hebrew infant into the Nile to drown, die of exposure, or be eaten by crocodiles (Exod. 1:22).

Scripture Reading..

"By faith Moses' parents hid him for three months after he was born, because they saw he was no ordinary child, and they were not afraid of the king's edict." —Hebrews 11:23

ACTS 7:17–21

Study and Reflection

1. Perhaps Shiphrah and Puah, or those under their supervision, spared Moses's older brother Aaron before Pharaoh put everyone in his population police. Now, Hebrew parents were commanded to abandon their babies in the Nile (Acts 7:19). How did Moses's parents show they weren't afraid to disobey the king's command? Do you think "not afraid" describes their emotions, actions, or both?

2. Apply this story to today. What does it mean to not fear someone or something, for example, bad news, an unjust boss, or a threatening diagnosis?

3. Think of an impossible situation you're facing or have faced. The Bible says, "When I am afraid, I put my trust in you" (Ps. 56:3). Note it says "when," not "if." Fear is an invitation to trust God. What do you take from the following to help you when you feel afraid?

   a. "Fearing people is a dangerous trap, but trusting the LORD means safety" (Prov. 29:25 NLT).

   b. "Dear friends, don't be afraid of those who want to kill your body; they cannot do any more to you after that. But I'll tell you whom to fear. Fear God, who has the power to kill you and then throw you into hell. Yes, he's the one to fear" (Luke 12:4–5 NLT).

   c. "But even if you suffer for doing what is right, God will reward you for it. So don't worry or be afraid of their threats. Instead, you must worship Christ as Lord of your life. And if someone asks about your hope as a believer, always be ready to explain it" (1 Pet. 3:14–15 NLT).

   d. "For God has not given us a spirit of fear and timidity, but of power, love, and self-discipline" (2 Tim. 1:7 NLT).

4.   Record your final thoughts or takeaways from today's lesson.

Those Who Revere God
*"Security is mostly a superstition. It does not exist in nature,
nor do the children of men as a whole experience it. Avoiding
danger is no safer in the long run than outright exposure.
Life is a daring adventure or nothing."* —Helen Keller

Have you seen people trade integrity for dollars and wisdom for cents over lesser matters than what the Hebrews faced? Those who walk in truth protect their souls and inspire others. Consider the examples below.

In Business
Some employees approached their CEO concerning a client's request to manipulate the findings in favor of a product they were researching. The CEO met with the client to flatly refuse their dishonest request and terminate their relationship. This leader sacrificed a valuable account to protect personal and company integrity.

In School
A high school teacher assigned her class opinion papers on current issues. A student researched and wrote a paper against abortion. The teacher scrawled a red *F* with a note across the paper: "You need to catch up with the times."

At Home
A teenager asked her youth group leader what she should do. Her church-attending parents wanted her to lie about her age to save a few dollars at the movie theater. How could she honor her parents and God?

In Challenging Circumstances

Are we helpless victims of our circumstances? John MacArthur wrote, "The course and the quality of our lives are determined much more by our decisions than by our circumstances."[3] The New Testament commends men and women who practiced their faith during opposition:

> Some faced jeers and flogging, and even chains and
> imprisonment. They were put to death by stoning;
> they were sawed in two; they were killed by the sword.
> They went about in sheepskins and goatskins, destitute,
> persecuted and mistreated—the world was not worthy
> of them. (Heb. 11:36–38)

Trials reveal the genuineness of our faith. Even before the Mosaic law, the Hebrews knew Pharaoh's edict to murder babies was wrong. The reason God forbade taking a human life had not changed (Gen. 9:5–6). The faith of the midwives and of Moses's parents sparkled under Pharaoh's cold cruelty. Our faith shines in darkness too.

The faith that supports us through momentous times is built on everyday choices. Who we are in private is who we are. Small decisions matter. I can't compromise in one area and not have it impact my character and destiny. God promises eternal rewards to those who hold fast. We guard every aspect of our lives because we never know through which gap the thief will enter.

A compromise in one area produces fallout in areas we can't predict or control. Let's decide today to be people of integrity before we're challenged. God sees and cares about our decisions whether anyone else applauds or not.

The Fear of God Removes the Fear of Man

Throughout history, egotistical leaders like Pharaoh have tried to cancel God's holy tenets. While the Bible teaches submission to government authorities, Scripture also teaches God established those authorities to serve him (Rom. 13:1–4). Every person—slave and free, ruler and ruled—will one day stand before him (Heb. 9:27). When those over us move out from under God's authority, we remain aligned under God (Acts 5:28–29). Doing so may draw fire. But remembering that we and those who threaten us will one day stand before God provides strength to resist unrighteous decrees (Rom. 14:10–12).

Thomas Jefferson held the motto, "Rebellion to tyrants is obedience to God." However, violating human authority may create a false sense of guilt. The student with the F grade mentioned above may feel unsettled. But heaven applauds her brave refusal to silence truth.

Some might argue she could accomplish more if she earned a scholarship. God controls our futures. The Bible promises, "Those who honor me I will honor, but those who despise me will be disdained" (1 Sam. 2:30). God gave families to the midwives and recorded their names in the Bible and the book of life. Moses's family experienced the Lord's favor. Thousands of years later, these faithful servants are still enjoying their reward.

Bolstering Our Courage

Around the world, people still suffer like the Hebrews in Egypt. When we arrived in what was then communist-ruled Poland, I gained an appreciation for persecution. Exactly one year earlier, government officers had turned AK-47s on peaceful demonstrators. They'd brutally beaten and killed many citizens. The night we arrived, we joined Warsaw's silent citizens who marked this bloody anniversary by carrying candles down streets lined on both sides by soldiers holding machine guns.

According to Open Doors USA, 360 million Christians suffer extensively for following Christ. That means one in seven believers worldwide suffers high levels of persecution for their faith.[4]

Anne Graham Lotz wrote,

> It has been estimated by the World Christian Encyclopedia that more than 45 million men and women were put to death for their faith in Jesus Christ during the twentieth century! In recent years the estimate has averaged between 160,000 and 171,000 per year. Imagine! That's more than 10,000 Christians dying for their faith every month! More than 400 per day![5]

I hope we never have to choose between life and what's right. But instead of fearing what might happen, let's strengthen ourselves by living strong today. Saying Scripture out loud and praying for those in trials bolsters my courage and peace when I'm tempted to worry.

It's normal to *feel* afraid. When we do, let's declare with the psalmist, "When I am afraid, I put my trust in you" (Ps. 56:3).

Today's Strength Builder

What authority figure can put you in a hard place? What helps you practice integrity in your predicament?

CLOSING PRAYER

Use this space to turn your insights and responses into prayers.

Day Three

Fear of God Makes a Fearless Mother

Jochebed means "Jehovah is glory."[6]

My child stares into the refrigerator. "Where's the mustard?"

"In the refrigerator."

"I don't see it."

I walk over and point.

"Oh."

Where did Jochebed get the idea to hide her baby in the place the Hebrews were told to discard their babies? Perhaps she knew hiding him in plain sight made him disappear. Picture the scene with me.

Jochebed caressed her baby's silky head, wondering if she'd ever see him again. She pressed her lips against his forehead before gently tucking a protective cloth over him to shield him from insects and the sun that would soon rise. *May the Lord cover you with his wings.* She hesitated before wading back to her daughter.

"Mother, you can't see the basket. The bulrushes hide it," young Miriam said.

Jochebed nodded, knowing a hungry tummy and a wet bottom would only too soon leave her son screaming. Jochebed stroked Miriam's curls. "Stay close to your brother, but don't be seen watching him," Jochebed whispered. "I'll slip back to feed him when I can. God be with you both."

~

Then Pharaoh gave this order to all his people: "Throw every newborn Hebrew boy into the Nile River. But you may let the girls live."

> About this time, a man and woman from the tribe
> of Levi got married. The woman became pregnant
> and gave birth to a son. She saw that he was a spe-
> cial baby and kept him hidden for three months. But
> when she could no longer hide him, she got a basket
> made of papyrus reeds and waterproofed it with tar
> and pitch. She put the baby in the basket and laid
> it among the reeds along the bank of the Nile River.
> (Exod. 1:22–2:3 NLT)

Jochebed hid her baby where others abandoned theirs. Maybe people had learned to tune out the sound of babies crying from the Nile. Perhaps she hoped the king wouldn't kill an older child if she could hide him a while longer. Or maybe she knew people overlooked the obvious.

Had Jochebed coached Miriam on what to say if someone found her son? Did Pharaoh's daughter usually bathe there? Had Jochebed observed a sympathetic nature in her? Was the princess part of Jochebed's plan? Even if the princess felt compassion for the baby, wouldn't her father heed his own command and have the baby killed?

Or was the arrival of the princess a shock? Had Jochebed hidden Moses, hoping *no one* would discover her son? Was Miriam terrified when the princess approached Moses's hiding place?

What about crocodiles? One could easily snatch a three-month-old baby. How could young Miriam save her brother from their jaws?

While God doesn't fill in these details, his involvement is obvious.

This Egyptian princess could easily have had one of her atten-dants dump Moses into the Nile. Instead, she chose to adopt him and pay Jochebed to care for him. This was better than Jochebed could have imagined!

But to save Moses, Jochebed would have to release him a second time once he was weaned. Her baby would live, but he would grow up in the house of her enemy. One who hated her God would educate him.

Each day Jochebed nursed Moses brought her one day closer to releasing him. Jochebed celebrated Moses's first steps with joy—and tears. Soon he would be Pharaoh's grandson. How, in this brief time, could she impart faith for a lifetime?

Moses later wrote, "Teach us to number our days, that we may gain a heart of wisdom" (Ps. 90:12). Perhaps Jochebed's example instilled this wisdom.

Moses's parents, Amram and Jochebed, came from the tribe of Levi (Exod. 2:1, 6:20; Num. 26:58–59). We know they succeeded in imparting their bold faith to their children: Moses, Aaron, and Miriam. These siblings became esteemed leaders in Israel. Moses became one of Israel's greatest prophets and leaders. God used him to deliver Israel from Egypt and to record the first five books of the Bible. We call the instructions God gave Israel for life and worship the law of Moses. Moses's older brother Aaron became Israel's high priest, and Miriam became a prophetess. Enjoy this family's amazing story of courageous faith.

Scripture Reading...
EXODUS 1:22–2:10

Study and Reflection

1. What did Moses's parents do when they faced the king's terrible edict (Exod. 2:1–10)?

2. How did God reward their faith?

3. It was customary to nurse a child until age three or four. To save Moses, Jochebed released him into her archenemy's care. How do you apply Jochebed's example to your life? What has God asked you to release into his care?

4. What motivated this couple? See Hebrews 11:6, 23.

5. According to James 1:5–8, what should we do when we face trials?

6. Record your final thoughts from today's lesson.

Trusting the Eternal Father

Kendra* stared at the pink line on her pregnancy test. This couldn't be happening. Single and still in school, she couldn't care for a child. But neither could she abort her baby.

After weeks of deliberation, she registered with an adoption agency. She poured over each applicant's file, seeking the perfect couple for her baby.

Stroking her swollen belly, Kendra called her caseworker to tell her the couple she'd chosen. "Please give them the news on Christmas Eve. I want them to always remember this baby is a gift."

---

*Names changed for anonymity.

As her due date approached, dread grew in Kendra's heart. Every kick from the baby reminded her of her pending delivery date. Could she let him go?

Three weeks before her due date, Kendra disappeared from the system. "That's not unusual," the caseworker said. "To give up the baby you've carried is like losing a limb."

Modern women who carry a child to term and entrust him/her into another's arms to nurture can identify with Jochebed at a depth most of us can't. Jochebed gave up her baby twice, first to the Nile and then to Pharaoh's daughter. But mothers aren't the only ones who suffer. In his book *Desperate for Hope*, Bruce W. Martin describes the bittersweet moment when the birth mother and grandfather of his adopted son said goodbye.

"After the grandfather said his goodbyes, he began sobbing. Not just crying, but sobbing, his lungs taking in great gulps of air, then expelling it in staccato heaves. He motioned for my wife to come near and tried to speak between sobs. Over and over again, he said, 'Please tell me you'll take good care of him. Please!'"[7]

The Bible doesn't elaborate on the toll turning Moses over to Pharaoh's daughter took on Jochebed, Moses, and the rest of the family. I believe an eternal perspective fortified them. They knew God was writing a story that stretched past their lifetimes. He had not forsaken them, and he would watch over Moses—even in enemy territory.

Today's Strength Builder

What has God called you to release? How does Jochebed help you?

CLOSING PRAYER

Use this space to turn your insights and responses into prayers.

Day Four

Fear of God Unleashes Supernatural Provision

The sound of breaking glass drew me to the living room where my toddler sat banging ceramic angels together and watching their bits fly. A couple of years later, I knew it would take a special couple to oversee my angel smasher and his sister if my husband and I accepted an invitation to spend ten days in Amsterdam ministering at a Billy Graham conference. Some trusted friends stepped up.

Our long flight from Los Angeles was delayed a few hours. I used the time to write postcards. This aggravating wait proved providential when the cards I sent from Europe didn't arrive until the day before our return. Every night, my homesick son asked to hear the note I'd mailed from the airport.

When Jochebed committed Moses to the Lord's keeping, she couldn't have imagined how God would work out his protection. For three months, she lived one day at a time, trying to keep him quiet and hidden. Each week he slept less and interacted more. When she could hide him no longer, she covered a papyrus basket with pitch and put her baby in the Nile River.

In an ironic twist, God took his chosen deliverer and hid him in the house of Satan's puppet. Pharaoh even provided Moses's education. I'm sure Jochebed prayed without ceasing for Moses. While the separation surely pained them both, she trusted God's hand.

Scripture Reading..
REVIEW EXODUS 2:1–10

Study and Reflection

1. In what ways do you identify with Jochebed?

2. What do you learn about God from this lesson?

3. Besides fearing for one's life, we can fear disappointing or angering others. How can fearing people trap you (Prov. 29:25)? How can trusting the Lord bring peace?

4. How does Jochebed's story help you? What do you learn from her?

5. Record any final thoughts from today's lesson.

Entrusting Our Children into the Father's Hands

"If a man harbors any sort of fear, it percolates through all his thinking, damages his personality, and makes him a landlord to a ghost." —Lloyd C. Douglas

What do these examples have in common?

- A conscientious parent sharing custody with an errant spouse

- An unwed mother giving her child for adoption
- A parent sending a child off to war

Candyce Carden, a military mom, woke one night fighting panic during her son's deployment to Fallujah with the US Marines during the height of the Iraq War. She prayed Scripture to calm herself. After someone robbed her nearby nephew at gunpoint, she realized children don't have to be at war seven thousand miles from home to meet danger. "No matter how near our children are, disaster can strike. Paradoxically, this recognition helped me let go of the fear that had gripped me during my son's deployment. Having my boy home wouldn't ensure his safety. I had to let go and trust God."[8]

The illusion of control feels good, but invariably, situations arise to remind us how little we have. We weary ourselves trying to manage our children in ways we weren't meant to. We struggle to protect them from hurt when we could release them into God's capable and loving hands.

Jochebed's stomach must have knotted when the midwife placed Moses in her arms. He was beautiful. But should she open her heart to a child she would lose? Jochebed and Amram accepted their son as a gift from God and committed him to God's care. God was bigger than their worst enemy and their greatest fear.

Jochebed trusted God one day at a time. She cared for her infant in secret. When he grew too big to hide at home, she made a little ark and placed him in the Nile. When Pharaoh's daughter paid her to nurse him, she nourished his soul as well as his body. When the time arrived to release him, she relied on God for the strength to follow through.

How did she—how can we—fight the concerns that surely taunted her? Isaiah 8:12–14 (NLT) says, "Don't live in dread of what frightens them. Make the LORD of Heaven's Armies holy in your life. He is the one you should fear. He is the one who should make you tremble. He will keep you safe."

Focus makes the difference. Jochebed understood her children belonged to God, not to her. She committed them and their outcomes to her big God, who loved them better than she. If soldiers stormed her house, what could she do? Instead of focusing on what she couldn't control, she poured herself into what she could—nurture her children in the Lord.

If a murderous king didn't intimidate Jochebed, then hostile forces need not scare us. If Jochebed could trust God to be with her child in her enemy's household, we can trust him to be with our loved ones in dangerous situations too.

Like Jochebed, when fear and dread threaten our peace, we can set our minds on the Lord. When awe of God replaces the fear of lesser things, he becomes our sanctuary—our safety, our peace. And from that place, we become all God intended. Jochebed's faith produced Moses, Aaron, and Miriam. What dread do you need to release?

Today's Strength Builder

Instead of focusing on what you can't do, in God's strength take the step he's laid before you.

CLOSING PRAYER

Use this space to turn your insights and responses into prayers.

Day Five

Released and Ready

"The horse is made ready for the day of battle,
but victory rests with the LORD."
—Proverbs 21:31

Two daughters, a Hebrew slave and an Egyptian princess, both play important roles in Moses's rescue and, in turn, Israel's deliverance. The royal princess enjoyed power and privilege. But with her position came the pressure to support the crown—the source of the Hebrews' hardship. Was she free to make her own decisions? Let's use our imagination to draw back the curtain of time and peek at the next scene.

Miriam braided marsh grass while she guarded her brother. The water gently rocked his little ark. She wished she could hold him. His newfound giggle enchanted her.

Approaching voices made her stiffen. Pharaoh's daughter and attendants strolled in the direction of her brother's hiding place. Her brother chose that moment to whimper.

The princess stopped and surveyed the marsh reeds. Spotting the basket, she motioned to a young attendant. "Bring me the basket."

The attendant waded in and returned, cradling the basket. Pharaoh's daughter peeled back the cloth cover. The whimper turned to wails. "One of the Hebrew babies," the princess whispered.

Noting the compassion on the princess's face, Miriam stepped forward and bowed. "Shall I get a Hebrew woman to nurse the baby for you?"

The princess hesitated only a moment, then nodded. "Yes, go."

Some believe this unnamed Egyptian princess was Pharaoh's only daughter. If so, was she a daddy's girl? I don't know what kind of father Pharaoh was to his daughter, but she knew about her father's coldhearted decree. Did she hope to soften him before the child was weaned?

Pharaoh's daughter appears to be single. She didn't consult a husband, her father, or her mother when she made the decision to adopt Moses. She no doubt knew they would not approve. But God-prompted compassion moved this idol-worshiper to protect this baby born to Hebrew slaves. She threw aside her father's prejudices and risked his chastening. She could not save all the babies, but she would rescue this one.

Throughout biblical history, God has moved secular leaders to help his people. This princess adopted Moses as her own child and educated God's future deliverer in the wisdom of the Egyptians.

While our culture obsesses over the details of the rich and famous, the Bible records the names of the midwife slaves and the members of Moses's family—and leaves the royal princess and her ruling father anonymous. Today we look at how God used two daughters—a slave and a princess—to save Moses.

Scripture Reading...

"But then a new king came to the throne of Egypt who knew nothing about Joseph. This king exploited our people and oppressed them, forcing parents to abandon their newborn babies so they would die. At that time Moses was born—a beautiful child in God's eyes. His parents cared for him at home for three months. When they had to abandon him, Pharaoh's daughter adopted him and raised him as her own son. Moses was taught all the wisdom of the Egyptians, and he was powerful in both speech and action." —Acts 7:18–22 (NLT)

REVIEW EXODUS 2:1–10; EXODUS 15:20–21
MICAH 6:4

Study and Reflection

1. What similarities and contrasts struck you about young Miriam and Pharaoh's daughter?

2. How did young Miriam demonstrate strength?

3. What moved the princess to disobey her father's edict (Exod. 2:6)?

4. Approximately eighty years after Miriam helped save Moses, she and Aaron reunited with him. What roles did Miriam play, and how does God remember her in Exodus 15:20–21 and Micah 6:4?

5. Considering the five females we studied this week (the midwives, Jochebed, Pharaoh's daughter, and Miriam), what spoke to you most and why?

6. Relate Proverbs 21:31, "The horse is made ready for the day of battle, but victory rests with the LORD," to Jochebed's plan to rescue baby Moses.

7. Record your final thoughts from today's lesson.

God's Unexpected Heroines

What raced through Miriam's mind when she heard her brother crying and saw the princess approaching? Was the idea to find a wet nurse a quick response to the princess's pity or part of her mother's plan?

Think of the responsibility this child carried. Miriam could watch and report what happened, but how could she protect her brother from human or reptilian foes? What would have happened if Miriam had gotten bored and wandered off? Was God entrusting the life of his chosen deliverer into the hands of a youngster?

Pharaoh's daughter approached. She knew about her father's murderous decree, but what did that have to do with her? She may have shrugged off a slave begging for help, but God set it up so she had to behold one of the babies her father had so carelessly sentenced to death. She heard his sobs and watched tears stream down his plump cheeks. The insulation she'd built around her heart dissolved. But what could she do?

Miriam's quick response provided an outlet for the princess's newfound compassion.

Dr. Beverly McMillan became an abortionist to protect women from botched abortions. She never considered the babies until one of the workers asked to watch as she picked through the parts she'd suctioned out to be sure she'd successfully completed the abortion.

When I showed her, this terrible sadness came over me.
For the first time, I saw a little boy. At 12 weeks old, we
could see his perfectly formed little arm and tiny bicep.

At that moment, I had a flashback; I could imagine my own son in my mind, with the same little arm, flexing his bicep, smiling at me. . . .

I shook myself. Five minutes ago, this was a perfectly beautiful little boy, and now he was in pieces. I never committed another abortion.[9]

Recognizing the humanity of the preborn child prompted Dr. McMillan to leave the abortion industry and speak on behalf of the unborn. Recognizing the humanity of baby Moses moved Pharaoh's daughter to boldly adopt this castaway. Abortion versus adoption. The difference between death and life.[10]

Jochebed's Mission

Perhaps picking up a family resemblance, the princess quickly employed Jochebed to care for Moses until he was weaned. This new position, nanny to the princess's son, no doubt freed Jochebed from her other slave duties so she could dedicate herself to the care of her children.

Jochebed praised Yahweh for this window of time with her son. How could she prepare him to resist the enemy and fulfill his calling in so little time? She filled each exchange with purpose. Instead of wallowing in self-pity or worrying over what might happen, Jochebed instilled into Moses, Aaron, and Miriam a love for God and an understanding of their calling as his chosen people. She left the outcome with God. The result? All three of her children became distinguished leaders in Israel.

God turned Jochebed's weakness, a slave bearing a son under Pharaoh's reign, into deliverance for Israel. The Jews viewed Moses as the greatest of all men; God communicated with him face-to-face (Num. 12:6–8). How might God use your weakness to accomplish more than you can imagine?

Today's Strength Builder

How can you get your "horse" ready for the day of battle? What outcome will you surrender to the Lord?

CLOSING PRAYER

Use this space to turn your insights and responses into prayers.

Prayer Requests

Strength to Obey God's Call

Moses means "drawing out (of the water)."[1]

"Moses." Jochebed straightened her son's tunic.

"Yes, Mama."

"Remember—"

"I know. I'm one of God's chosen, and Yahweh can whip Pharaoh's gods." Moses swung his small fist.

"Yes, my son." Jochebed smiled.

"Mama?" Moses's sharp eyes searched hers. "When will I see you?"

Jochebed's breath caught, and she drew her son close and inhaled his clean scent. She recalled the princess's compassion and God's surprising provision. "I don't know. One day. One day, we'll gather together in the land God promised our father, Abraham."

~

The time came for Jochebed to release Moses. Would she ever see her son again? I can't imagine leaving my child in the care of someone who hated my people and my God.

What must this separation have been like for Moses? His mother wouldn't hear his calls in the night. His older brother and sister couldn't defend him. No matter how much his mother tried to prepare him, this separation must have shaken the whole family.

Day One
Called to a Greater Kingdom

People say hindsight is 20/20. But God offers something better than hindsight—the promise to work all things together for the good of those who love him (Rom. 8:28). That means one day we'll look back over our lives and see how God used every loss and pain for our benefit.

Jonathan Cahn says for God's children, "there are only two realities . . . blessings . . . and blessings in disguises."[2] After years of confusion, God gave my friend Susie spiritual eyes to recognize his protection in her losses.

Unlike Moses, Susie was born into a prosperous home. Cooks, housekeepers, and chauffeurs tended her family. But her life turned upside down when her parents sent her first to boarding school at the tender age of twelve and then halfway around the world to a girl's prep school in the United States at age sixteen. Susie spoke no English. Like Moses, she received the best in education and amenities—everything but what she wanted most: her family.

Between school sessions, when her classmates returned to their families, Susie attended camp. On rare visits from her father, she begged him to take her home. But he slipped away without a good-bye. She never understood why, out of her large family, her father sent only her to America. The opportunities her school and camp offered couldn't ease her homesickness.

Susie married an American. When she visited her family in their homeland, she felt like an outsider. One day, a neighbor invited Susie over for coffee. She introduced Susie to Jesus. Susie discovered a new family—the family of faith.

Susie believed God brought her to America to find Jesus. She became a missionary to her extended family, gently pointing them to the joy of knowing her Savior. She believed her temporary separation from her family would result in an eternal reunion in heaven. That hope strengthened her through many trials, including cancer.

With new eyes, Susie saw how her heavenly Father orchestrated the painful separation for her protection. Her youngest brother, who shared her sensitive nature, committed suicide at age sixteen. "I don't think I would have survived the cutthroat atmosphere of my home," Susie said.[3]

To save Moses's life, God placed him in Pharaoh's household. Torn from his God-fearing family, this preschooler moved from physical poverty to material luxury and from an atmosphere of spiritual light to one of spiritual darkness.

In his book *Desperate for Hope*, Bruce Martin wrote, "God is more intent on perfecting us through trouble than protecting us from trouble."[4] That rings true for many of God's chosen people, both biblical and modern. Through no fault of their own, many land in a crucible.

Hindsight allows us to see how God used trouble to complete Susie and Moses. Perhaps the contrast in Moses's homes put the riches of Egypt in perspective. Like Susie's situation, no material luxury could fill the hole in Moses's aching heart. He loathed Pharaoh's brutality and lived as an outsider in his Egyptian family. Susie and Moses shared a desire to save their people. Their trials produced something better than hindsight—an eternal perspective with the foresight to recognize the value of knowing Jesus.

Scripture Reading...

"By faith Moses, when he had grown up, refused to be known as the son of Pharaoh's daughter. He chose to be mistreated along with the people of God rather than to enjoy the fleeting pleasures of sin. He regarded disgrace for the sake of Christ as of greater value than the treasures of Egypt, because he was looking ahead to his reward." —Hebrews 11:24–26

"For our light and momentary troubles are achieving for us an eternal glory that far outweighs them all. So we fix our eyes not on what is seen, but on what is unseen, since what is seen is temporary, but what is unseen is eternal." —2 Corinthians 4:17–18

"What good is it for someone to gain the whole world, yet forfeit their soul?" —Mark 8:36

Study and Reflection

1. Why did Moses choose to align himself with God's people when doing so meant losing the comforts of palace life and drawing Pharaoh's wrath?

2. Apply Moses's example to your life. What helps you persevere through hard decisions?

3. How did an eternal perspective help Moses (2 Cor. 4:17–18; Mark 8:36)?

4. Sin offers temporary pleasure and lasting regret. Sin encompasses more than indulging base desires. It's falling short of God's glory. To stay in the palace after God called Moses to leave was to indulge in "the passing pleasures of sin." How might remembering that sin's consequences outlast its pleasures help you (Heb. 11:25)?

5. Record any final thoughts or takeaways from today's lesson.

A Man Is Known by the Treasure He Seeks

I've never understood the phrase "to die for" regarding material possessions. If you're dead, what good are those to-die-for shoes? The ancient Egyptians took this to a whole new level.

King Tut's tomb provides a glimpse into the immense affluence of Egypt's royal family. The tomb's treasures include a gilded fan, elaborate jewelry, a golden throne, and three coffins, one of solid gold—and a pair of to-die-for gold sandals.[5]

For nearly forty years, Moses lived the life of the rich and famous while his fellow Hebrews struggled to survive. God placed him in Pharaoh's palace to save his life and train him. But God didn't plant him there. Hundreds of years earlier, God placed Joseph, another Hebrew slave, in another pharaoh's palace to save Israel (Ps. 105). But God had a different plan for Moses.

The late minister J. Vernon McGee believes Moses "would have been the next pharaoh."[6] If not the next pharaoh, he would surely have held a position of influence. But that wouldn't have accomplished God's plan. Moses couldn't deliver God's people from inside the palace. What incentive would the Hebrews have had to go to the Promised Land if Moses ruled Egypt?

Indignation at the cruelty Moses witnessed built within him. The seeds Jochebed had sown into his young heart sprouted into compassion for his people. Moses couldn't keep one foot in the palace and another with the Hebrews. He had to choose.

Someone once quipped that the only thing in the middle of a highway is roadkill. If you want to be miserable, try to keep one foot in the world and one in Christ. Moses "regarded disgrace for the sake of Christ as of greater value than the treasures of Egypt."

This fitting evaluation led Moses to choose mistreatment "along with the people of God rather than to enjoy the fleeting pleasures of sin" (Heb. 11:25–26).

Regarding Moses, Charles R. Swindoll wrote,

We must refuse to go with the flow of a sinful society (11:24–26). Anyone today who encounters the deteriorating moral values of the world will have to decide between two paths—one leading deeper into Egypt, the other toward the Promised Land. We face this decision not only once or twice in our lives, but daily . . . over and over again.[7]

When Moses found his to-die-for treasure, he left the royal palace but not his princely calling. Rabbi Jonathan Cahn wrote, "Those who are truly royal have no need of crowns or thrones. Their royalty is found not in what lies around them but what lies within them."[8]

If Moses had stayed in the palace, history would have forgotten him. Moses couldn't have imagined the significance this choice would have on him and all of history. Humanly speaking, if Moses had chosen Egypt, the rest of Hebrews 11 wouldn't have happened. Today, biblical and secular accounts herald him as one of the greatest leaders of all time.

Today's Strength Builder

To identify with God's people, Moses had to stop being known as Pharaoh's grandson. What family values did you have to leave (or need to leave) to fully follow Christ (Heb. 11:24–25)?

CLOSING PRAYER

Use this space to turn your insights and responses into prayers.

Day Two

Called to Do God's Will God's Way

When the Lord called me into vocational Christian work, I expected pushback from some family members. But I never predicted one would contact my friends and extended family and tell them not to support me.

Moses expected his Egyptian family to ridicule his aligning with the Hebrew slaves. But surely, the Hebrews would embrace him. His status, education, and oratory skills made him their perfect deliverer. Or so he must have thought. But God couldn't use Moses while he relied on himself.

Bible teacher Dr. Ken Boa says Moses spent the first forty years of his life being a somebody, the second forty years being a nobody, and the last forty years learning God uses nobodies.

Moses must have felt like a big zero when his own people rejected him. How could he have blown his chance to help them? Just as your teen needs practice behind the wheel as well as schooling in safety and driving laws before you let him loose with your car, after palace training, Moses needed desert training.

God had work to do in Moses to make him a leader greater than any pharaoh. God's preparation took longer and was more difficult than Moses could have fathomed. But the reward was more lasting and magnificent than he could have hoped for. Thousands of years later, Moses would stand with Elijah to minister to God's

Son at the transfiguration. But before that could happen, Moses had to learn to pursue God's goal, God's way, in God's timing.

Scripture Reading..
ACTS 7:22–36

Study and Reflection

1. How did Moses try to rescue his people (Acts 7:23–29)?

2. Have you ever set off to right a wrong, and things did not work out as you pictured? "Moses assumed his fellow Israelites would realize that God had sent him to rescue them, but they didn't" (Acts 7:25 NLT). How might this set-back have affected him (Acts 7:25–29)?

3. Acts 7 divides Moses's life into three forty-year segments. In Egypt, he became powerful in speech and action (v. 22). In Midian, he learned survival training living as a foreigner and a fleeing refugee (v. 29). In the desert, he performed signs and wonders, was a prophet who received living words from an angel, and a leader of obstinate people (vv. 36–39). His life-time of experiences snapped together to shape God's chosen deliverer for Israel. God didn't waste one day. Yet, during the middle forty-year stretch, Moses probably felt sidelined. Has a long wait ever made you question God's calling for your life? Does Moses's story encourage you? Why or why not?

4. How did Moses know when to return to Egypt (Acts 7:30–36)?

5. God's plan, when pursued my way, won't work. Why do we try to insert our methods or timing into God's plan (Prov. 3:5–6)?

6. Record your final thoughts from today's lesson.

I Found Something Better than Working for God
"The messes in life are my best teachers; I don't like them, but I need them." —Cecil Murphy

My son introduced esophagus strips to our standard poodles. Now they turn up their noses at other treats. I discovered Dark Chocolate covered almonds. That's become my favorite pick-me-up. Moses discovered something better than working *for* God.

Working for God can leave us disillusioned. When we strive *for* God, we make mistakes in "his name." We bruise people and become resentful, proud, or worn out. Instead of building his kingdom, we hinder it.

Moses thought he worked for God when he murdered an Egyptian taskmaster. Saul of Tarsus thought he worked for God when he threw Christians into prison. The Pharisees and religious leaders believed they worked for God when they crucified God's Son (Mark 14:64).

A Better Way
What's better than working *for* Jesus (Acts 17:25)? Working *with* him (1 Cor. 3:9). Those who work *for* God ask him to bless their

ideas. Those who work *with* God join him in his plan. They look to him for guidance and strength. He leads; they follow.

- Moses learned to rely on God. "Then Moses said to him, 'If your Presence does not go with us, do not send us up from here'" (Exod. 33:15).
- Saul of Tarsus was transformed into the apostle Paul, who said, "My old self has been crucified with Christ. It is no longer I who live, but Christ lives in me. So I live in this earthly body by trusting in the Son of God, who loved me and gave himself for me" (Gal. 2:20 NLT).
- Jesus said, "I no longer call you servants. . . . Instead, I have called you friends, for everything that I learned from my Father I have made known to you" (John 15:15), and "Yes, I am the vine; you are the branches. Those who remain in me, and I in them, will produce much fruit. For apart from me you can do nothing" (John 15:5 NLT).

I used to beat myself up when I failed to meet my expectations. I'm learning my job is to follow the Holy Spirit's leading. Moses lived in the desert forty years before God said it was time to move. Waiting on Jesus takes faith. But faith is the work that pleases God (John 6:28–29).

When we serve God by working with him, he gets the glory. His plan is to build his kingdom, through his power, in his time.

Four Ways to Work with God

Consider the following in light of a current project or role:

1. Ask God to show you if and where you've substituted self-effort for faith.
2. Admit your inadequacy and surrender your will, your way, and your timetable to God.

3. Ask God to fill you with his Spirit and teach you to rely on him in every area of your life. Turn away from self-effort and choose faith. If you trust him in every area but one, you're still striving.
4. Thank him for leading and equipping you.

Who makes a better ambassador for Christ, the one who works for God or the one who works with him? Once we've experienced God in our work, why would we ever settle for striving in our own strength?

Today's Strength Builder

While God uses our passions, talents, and training, he wants us to depend on him. Choose to rely on God today instead of your skills, plans, or experience.

CLOSING PRAYER

Use this space to turn your insights and responses into prayers.

Day Three
Called to Trust God

If things were bad for the Hebrews when Moses fled Egypt, they only grew worse in his forty-year absence. Author Bruce Martin says, "It can always get worse." To prove his point, Martin points to Job. He could have pointed to Moses.

The Great I AM

I pressed my cheek against my infant daughter's and smiled at her reflection in the mirror. My smile dropped. Next to her newborn cheeks my twenty-seven-year-old skin looked ancient.

When God revealed himself to Moses in the burning bush, Moses trembled and hid his face. Glimpsing the Lord's glory flattened Isaiah and Peter too (Isa. 6:5; Luke 5:8). Before commissioning these men, the Lord revealed his holiness. Next to his purity, their flaws glared like strobe lights.

Moses's exchange with God at the burning bush humbled Moses and revealed God's trustworthiness and superiority over every other religion. Unlike detached pagan gods, the God of Abraham wanted a personal relationship with his people.

The God of Israel:

- Saw Israel's oppression, heard their cries, and called Moses by name.
- Is holy. "You are on holy ground."
- Communicated in a way Moses understood.
- Cared for his people.

Scripture remembers Moses as one powerful in word and deed (Acts 7:22). But at the burning bush, Moses rehearsed his inadequacies. Did God see something Moses couldn't see in himself? Or was God resurrecting the talent and training that had lain dormant for forty years?

Despite Moses's reservations and the prior fiasco of killing the Egyptian, God wouldn't accept his no. Anticipating Moses's reluctance, God had already summoned Aaron to accompany Moses before commissioning him (Exod. 4:14–15).

God switched Moses's focus from "Who am I?" to the great "I AM." God had never planned for Moses to deliver the nation in his own strength. Moses had gotten it wrong the first time. This time

God would lead. Yahweh would accomplish his mission through his chosen instrument. What a difference for Moses—and for us. God uses our past failures to teach us to rely on him (2 Cor. 12:9).

Scripture Reading..
EXODUS 2:11–4:22

Study and Reflection

1. The burdens we feel are clues to God's calling. Moses apparently felt compassion for underdogs, as shown on two recorded occasions (Exod. 2:11–19). What issues or situations stir your heart?

2. God said, "Moses! Moses!" Repeating someone's name was the Hebrew way of showing intimacy. Perhaps Moses felt overlooked during his four decades in the desert. Had God forgotten his kinsmen in Egypt? What does this scene reveal about God (Exod. 3:1–10)?

3. Before calling Simon Peter, an experienced fisherman, to fish for men, Jesus displayed his power over fish. When Peter saw the catch, "he fell at Jesus' knees and said, 'Go away from me, Lord; I am a sinful man!'" (Luke 5:8). When Moses "heard the Lord say: 'I am the God of your fathers, the God of Abraham, Isaac and Jacob.' Moses trembled with fear and did not dare to look. Then the Lord said to him, 'Take off your sandals, for the place where you are standing is holy ground'"

(Acts 7:31–33). Why do you think God orchestrated these encounters before commissioning these men?

4. God told Abraham his descendants would be oppressed in a foreign land for four hundred years. Afterward, they would come out and worship him in the Promised Land (Gen. 15:13; Acts 7:6–7). God chose Moses to be his instrument of deliverance. How did God use language that appealed to Moses's gift of compassion (Exod. 3:7–10; Acts 7:34)?

5. Self-confidence and self-doubt both revolve around *self* and undercut God-confidence. A strong sense of indignation moved Moses to push ahead of God. His confidence collapsed after failure. To get over himself, Moses had to focus on God (Exod. 3:11; 4:1, 10–20).

    a. In what situations are you more likely to let feelings rule you?

    b. How did God answer Moses's excuses, "Who am I that I should go?" (Exod. 3:11–15)?

6. God had anticipated Moses's concerns (Exod. 4:13–17). How do you apply this to your challenges?

7. What additional thoughts do you have about Moses or from the reading?

A Sure Way to Success

"It is not that we think we are qualified to do anything on our own. Our qualification comes from God." —2 Corinthians 3:5 NLT

A wonderful conference inspired me but left me feeling out of place. The younger participants were light-years ahead of me in their knowledge of technology and social media. I felt like I'd pulled up to a jet-fueling station in a horse and buggy. While their spaceships intrigued me, I wasn't sure I could—or wanted to—drive one.

Focusing on our limitations magnifies them. Exodus 4:11 says, "The LORD said to [Moses], 'Who gave human beings their mouths? Who makes them deaf or mute? Who gives them sight or makes them blind? Is it not I, the LORD?'"

Remembering God's sovereignty over my inherent weaknesses helps me forget them. In God's economy, my abilities don't enhance his chance of success. But focusing on my faults can hinder his work in and through me.

In *Made to Stick*, Dan and Chip Heath tell a story that illustrates the paralyzing effect of a negative self-perception.[9] After Martin Luther King Jr.'s assassination, a third-grade teacher wondered how she could help her class grasp the tragedy of prejudice. One morning she told her class that brown eyes were better than blue. She moved the blue-eyed students to the back of the room. They wore collars so their classmates could recognize them from a distance. Brown eyes enjoyed a longer recess.

Friendships dissolved as brown-eyed children shunned their blue-eyed peers. The next day, she told the class she'd made a mistake. Blue eyes were superior to brown. The blue-eyed children squealed with delight and ran to put their collars around their brown-eyed classmates. The blue-eyed children completed their spelling drills faster that day.

"Why were you so slow yesterday?" she asked.

"Because all I could think about was those collars," one blue-eyed student said.

A Self-Defeating Focus
Is it possible to be biased against ourselves?

- While the third graders focused on their collars, they couldn't spell.
- While I focused on my lack of technical knowledge, I couldn't learn.
- While Moses focused on his limitations, he couldn't heed God's call.

At forty, Moses was comfortable in the Egyptian court. God's call would have made sense—then. But now? After forty years of herding sheep? The Egyptians despised shepherds. Pharaoh would certainly ridicule Moses and his demands.

God's calling usually requires courage. Like Moses, our excuses feel sensible. "I don't know enough. Others can do a better job." Or, "Let someone with more time and energy do it." If we're not careful, we'll spend the first half of our lives thinking we need more experience and the last half feeling outdated.

This mission wasn't about Moses—his strengths or weaknesses. He'd tripped over his strengths earlier. He needed to shed his self-sufficiency and discover God's sufficiency. While Moses focused on his inadequacy, he still focused on himself.

A New Focus

When Moses asked, "*Who am I*," he fixated on the wrong question. It wasn't about Moses. The great I AM would accomplish this (Exod. 3:7–10).

Jesus calls believers his ambassadors. If we focus on ourselves, we're in danger of puffing up in pride or shrinking back in fear. Jesus overlooked the trained religious leaders and chose a tax collector and fishermen to be his disciples. He interrupted Saul's rampage against the church to make him an apostle to the Gentiles.

The Scottish author George MacDonald significantly influenced the great writer and thinker C. S. Lewis. Ironically, Lewis wrote, "If we define Literature as an art whose medium is words, then certainly MacDonald has no place in its first rank—perhaps not even in its second."[10] Lewis respected the wisdom and holiness MacDonald's writings captured—not his writing ability.

If MacDonald had waited to share his wisdom until he was more proficient in crafting his thoughts, the profound influence he's had on my life and Lewis's would have been lost. Lewis's observation endeared MacDonald to me even more. If we submit ourselves to God, he uses us for his glory. As the saying goes, "God doesn't choose us based on our ability but on our availability."

Remember the boy who offered his lunch of five loaves and two fish to Jesus when thousands were hungry (John 6:1–14)? Andrew saw the lunch and said, "But what are these for so many people?" Yet, Jesus fed five thousand plus with that small offering. When we offer what we have, Jesus makes it enough.

No one is adequate to serve Christ. But, like the third graders who shed their collars, we can lay aside our insufficiencies and set our eyes on Jesus. On what will you focus, "Who am I?" or "the great I AM"?

Today's Strength Builder

Have you offered Jesus all of you—including your fears and flaws? Try it and invite the Holy Spirit to fill every aspect of your life.

CLOSING PRAYER

Use this space to turn your insights and responses into prayers.

Day Four

Called to Keep the Passover

Moses's heading off to confront Pharaoh reminds me of a scene from the movie *The Princess Bride*. After evil Prince Humperdinck kills noble Wesley, Wesley's friends carry their lifeless hero to Miracle Max in search of a miracle. Reluctantly, Max concocts a pill to revive the "mostly dead" Wesley so he can rescue Princess Buttercup from Humperdinck. As Wesley's two hopeful companions drag limp Wesley away to storm the castle, Max's wife mumbles, "Think it'll work?"

Waving to the departing young men, Max mumbles, "It'll take a miracle."

God told Moses it would take a miracle to deliver the Hebrews from Pharaoh. But, unlike Miracle Max, God specializes in miracles. God turned Pharaoh's stubbornness from a setback to a setup that displayed God's glory and raised the esteem of Moses in the eyes of the Egyptians and the Hebrews.

Hebrews 11 skips the first nine plagues to focus on the final one. No longer spectators, in the tenth plague, each Hebrew household was instructed to slaughter a lamb and use the blood to coat their doorframes. Their firstborns' lives depended on their obedience.

The celebration of the Passover became a lasting ordinance for Israel. The Passover pointed to the cross where God offered the Lamb of God for the salvation of the whole world. Paul wrote, "For the message of the cross is foolishness to those who are perishing, but to us who are being saved it is the power of God" (1 Cor. 1:18). That night, everyone who refused to follow God's instructions lost their firstborns. But everyone who applied the blood was spared.

The slaughter of a lamb demonstrated two deep truths: a parent's love for their child and God's love for us. "For God so loved the world that he gave his one and only Son, that whoever believes in him shall not perish but have eternal life" (John 3:16). As you read about the Passover, remember the greater miracle—the blood of God's Lamb rescues us from sin and Satan's power.

Scripture Reading..

"It was by faith that Moses commanded the people of Israel to keep the Passover and to sprinkle blood on the doorposts so that the angel of death would not kill their firstborn sons." —Hebrews 11:28 (NLT)

EXODUS 11–12

Study and Reflection

1. Record your thoughts on today's scripture reading.

2. According to Exodus 11:7–9, how would God work Pharaoh's stubbornness for good?

3. The Passover marked a new beginning for Israel. Jonathan Cahn says the Hebrew year had two calendars, the secular and the sacred. The sacred calendar began in the spring on the month of their deliverance (Exod. 12:2, 14, 17–18, 24–27). It correlates with Easter when the death of our Passover lamb, Messiah, "ushers in the springtime of your life, your new beginning, your second and sacred calendar."[11] Exodus 12:3 provides "the first continuous command given to the nation of Israel."[12] Before he gave Moses the Ten Commandments, God gave Israel the command to take a lamb on the tenth of Nisan. This pointed to Jesus in a remarkable way that wouldn't be understood until thousands of years later. On this exact day, "Messiah, the Lamb of God was taken to Jerusalem on the day we know as Palm Sunday."[13] Passover became a lasting ordinance for generations to come, a day to commemorate and celebrate "as a festival to the LORD." In the Bible, leaven often represents sin. At the Last Supper, Jesus explained the meaning of the unleavened bread, "This is my body given for you" (Luke 22:19). It represented his sinless body, broken for our sin. What purpose did the blood on their doorframes serve (Exod. 12:12–13, 23)?

4. God executed judgment on the gods of Egypt (Exod. 12:12). Some believe "gods" refers to spiritual forces behind Egyptian idol worship. The term could indicate human rulers since the Egyptians regarded Pharaoh as a god (Num. 33:3–4;

Ps. 82:1–2). The Egyptians worshiped animals like bulls and goats, the same animals God struck dead as part of the final plague. What happened to those who did not apply the lamb's blood (Exod. 12:29–30)?

5. 1 Corinthians 5:7 calls Christ our Passover lamb that was slaughtered. The Passover lamb died in place of the livestock and firstborn sons of those who followed Moses's instructions. Those who applied the blood and stayed up fretting were no more secure than those who applied the blood and rested. Obedient faith in God's prescribed way saved them. How do you apply this to our salvation (1 John 5:12–13)?

6. What additional thoughts do you have from the lesson or the reading?

Called to Rest in God's Provision

I googled, "How long a wait between coats of paint?" One search said, there is no time marker for how long between coats of paint: just make sure the previous coat has gone past the "tacky" stage. In mile-high Colorado, paint dried in one hour. In Boston, the drying process required three hours on some days.[14]

How many times have I botched a project because I rushed? My patient husband asked me early in our marriage to please leave the painting to him. Many tasks require waiting. Hurrying creates a mess.

Pharaoh's refusal to let the Hebrews go didn't surprise God. At the burning bush, God told Moses that Pharaoh wouldn't cooperate

(Exod. 3:19–22). The Egyptian ruler's stubbornness showcased God's power (Isa. 45:21–22). Centuries earlier, God told Abraham he'd punish the *nation* that mistreated his descendants. The nation, not just Pharaoh, had oppressed Israel and killed their babies.

> Then the LORD said to [Abraham], "Know for certain that for four hundred years your descendants will be strangers in a country not their own and that they will be enslaved and mistreated there. But I will punish the nation they serve as slaves, and afterward they will come out with great possessions." (Gen. 15:13–14)

Centuries before this scenario began, the Lord knew how long Israel would live in Egypt, that Egypt's ruler would turn against her, and how God would deliver his chosen people from slavery. God knew Pharaoh wouldn't release Israel until his firstborn son died.

> This is what the LORD says: Israel is my firstborn son, and I told you, "Let my son go, so he may worship me." But you refused to let him go; so I will kill your firstborn son. (Exod. 4:22–23)

If Egypt had repented, think of the suffering they would have avoided. Thousands of years later, we remember this showdown and marvel at God's patience and power. Plague after relentless plague did not soften Pharaoh's hard heart. Instead, he hardened it even when his stubborn defiance resulted in the destruction of his kingdom, the Egyptian people, and his own son.

One Coat of Blood

In this last plague, the death angel passed over every house with lamb's blood. Only one coat of lamb's blood was needed. Some Israelites may have watched their children sleep, worrying their blood-coated doors were not enough. Others painted their doors and rested.

Which homes were spared? The ones brushed with blood. The blood signaled that a lamb had died in place of their firstborn and told the angel the household belonged to God. The act of sacrificing the lamb and applying its blood to their doorframe reminded Israel to trust God.

God saved *every* family that applied the blood. Obedient faith in God's promise, not the state of their nerves, saved them. Pharaoh believed his gods and his guards would protect his household. But great faith in man-made idols could not deliver from death. It's not the strength of our trust but the object of our faith that matters. Faith in false gods equaled no faith in the true God. Warren Wiersbe wrote, "The issue is clear: faith means life, unbelief means death."[15]

Human power cannot stop death. That night, every household tasted loss—either a lamb or a son died. The Passover lamb depicts Jesus Christ's substitutionary death on the cross. Those who trust Jesus's blood to cover their sins will escape eternal death. Those who don't will suffer eternal death and separation from God.

How Do We Apply the Passover?

Pharaoh's calloused heart held one soft spot: his son. To spare us from eternal death, God offered his only Son. "For God did not send his Son into the world to condemn the world, but to save the world through him. Whoever believes in him is not condemned, but whoever does not believe stands condemned already because they have not believed in the name of God's one and only Son" (John 3:17–18).

Anyone who stood at the door to combat the death angel lost that battle. The blood, not their efforts, saved them. How do we apply the lamb's blood over our doorframes? By grace through faith.

> For by grace you have been saved through faith; and this is not of yourselves, it is the gift of God; not a result of works, so that no one may boast. (Eph. 2:8–9 NASB)

Christ died for our sins at the same time the Passover lambs were being slain in Jerusalem. He died in our place as the first Passover lambs died in place of Israel's firstborns (Isa. 53:4–5). His blood covers every sin the moment we place our faith in his death, burial, and resurrection. This includes your past, present, and future sins. After all, all your sins were in the future when Jesus died.

At the final judgment, if God were to ask you why he should let you into his heaven, how would you answer (Heb. 9:27)? Would you say you tried to live a good life? Your good deeds outweighed your bad?

There is only one acceptable answer: I've trusted the blood of the Lamb to cover my sins. If the sacrifice of a lamb could save Israel's firstborns, how much more will the blood of God's Lamb save us? If a past sin continues to taunt you, remember Jesus's blood. Thank God, our salvation rests on the blood of the Lamb—not on how well we paint.

Today's Strength Builder

Have you applied the blood of our Passover Lamb to your sin? If not, why not ask him to be your Lord and Savior and make you into the person he wants you to be? Thank Jesus today for dying in your place. Then rest in the power of his blood. Let this be your new beginning.

CLOSING PRAYER

Use this space to turn your insights and responses into prayers.

Day Five

Caught between the Devil and the Red Sea

*"What a paradox: Moses's life was saved by water,
and Pharaoh's army was destroyed by water."[16]*
—Warren W. Wiersbe

My friend gasped when her standard poodle grabbed a backyard rabbit. The bunny squealed like a baby. "Drop it," she screamed. The dog obeyed.

The rabbit showed no visible signs of injury. Relieved, she nudged the animal to move. But the rabbit had died from a heart attack.

Fear can be more deadly than what we fear.

Remember the phrase, "Caught between the devil and the deep blue sea," used to describe an impossible situation? Perhaps it came from today's reading. Fear swept through Israel like a tornado when they found themselves trapped between Pharaoh and the Red Sea.

Pharaoh had finally released Israel—but the battle wasn't over. The Lord led Israel with a pillar of cloud by day and a pillar of fire by night. He showed them where to camp and forewarned them of Pharaoh's next move. Sure enough:

> Pharaoh harnessed his chariot and called up his troops.
> He took with him 600 of Egypt's best chariots, along
> with the rest of the chariots of Egypt, each with its
> commander. . . . The Egyptians chased after them with
> all the forces in Pharaoh's army—all his horses and

chariots, his charioteers, and his troops. The Egyptians
caught up with the people of Israel as they were
camped beside the shore near Pi-hahiroth, across from
Baal-zephon. (Exod. 14:6–7, 9 NLT)

Israel reached the Red Sea and saw dust clouds from Pharaoh's
chariots approaching at an alarming speed. They were trapped.
Some cried out to the Lord. Others blasted Moses. "But Moses told
the people, 'Don't be afraid. Just stand still and watch the LORD
rescue you today. The Egyptians you see today will never be seen
again. The LORD himself will fight for you. Just stay calm'" (Exod.
14:13–14 NLT).

Unlike the bunny, Moses didn't fear Pharaoh's throng of chariots. Wiersbe said, "Moses was not afraid of the king's anger (v. 27),
the king's authority (v. 28), or the king's army (v. 29)."[17] Today, we
look at Moses's departure from Egypt, God's stunning rescue, and
the parting of the Red Sea.

Scripture Reading..

"It was by faith that Moses left the land of Egypt, not fearing the king's
anger. He kept right on going because he kept his eyes on the one who
is invisible.... It was by faith that the people of Israel went right through
the Red Sea as though they were on dry ground. But when the Egyptians
tried to follow, they were all drowned." —Hebrews 11:27, 29 (NLT)

EXODUS 13:17–14:31

Study and Reflection

1. Here is a mystery. God chose wicked Pharaoh to rule over
   Egypt. "For Scripture says to Pharaoh: 'I raised you up for
   this very purpose, that I might display my power in you

and that my name might be proclaimed in all the earth'"
(Rom. 9:17). How do you apply this to today?

2. Hundreds of years before this exodus, Joseph believed God
   would keep his promise to Abraham and bring his people out
   of Egypt into the Promised Land (Heb. 11:22). Pharaoh forgot
   Joseph, but Moses remembered him (Exod. 13:19). Moses
   believed God would bring Israel into the Promised Land. The
   Lord led Israel on their journey (Exod. 13:21–22). While the
   people saw the pillars of cloud and fire, who did Moses see
   (Heb. 11:27)? Relate this to Hebrews 11:1.

3. God had Israel turn back to draw Pharaoh out (Exod. 14:1–
   4). Why did God draw Pharaoh out and put Israel in this
   tight spot? How did this benefit Israel (Exod. 14:31)?

4. Apply this to a situation you face. Why might God have
   allowed your problem? Who might benefit?

5. The unbelieving Egyptians followed the Israelites through the
   Red Sea. The path that saved Israel destroyed the Egyptian
   army. What differentiated the two groups (Heb. 11:29)? How
   can you apply this when your path looks risky?

6. Israel's descriptive victory song in Exodus 15:1–21 credits God with winning the battle against Pharaoh and his chariots. Record any final thoughts or takeaways from today's lesson.

When All Seems Lost

The Egyptian army watched two million Israelites, including ancients and infants, hike across the expansive swath of land the east wind had carved through the middle of the sea. If the walls of water didn't intimidate slaves, then the king's finest soldiers wouldn't hold back. They reached the middle of the sea, and confusion broke out. Horses reared, wheels swerved, and chariots bogged. After ten plagues, the Egyptians finally connected the dots. "Let's get away from the Israelites! The LORD is fighting for them against Egypt" (Exod. 14:25).

With a roar, walls of saltwater collapsed, drowning Pharaoh's soldiers. Not one remained.

Notice, Israel followed God through the sea. The Egyptians followed Israel. The Hebrew God was not their God, and they were not his people. They didn't enter the Red Sea by faith.

Hanging out with Christians won't make you one any more than listening to arias makes me an opera singer. We need a personal relationship with Christ. There is a big difference between following Christ and following Christians.

Even believers aren't all called to walk the exact same path. We must turn off autopilot and seek God's guidance. Am I developing a personal relationship with Jesus? Have I learned to recognize his voice? Are my choices based on faith, or am I blindly following the crowd?

Faith to Trust

Ironically, God didn't just allow this face-off; he orchestrated it to show the world he is Lord. That problem you're facing, the one that's hemmed you in between a devil and a deep pit, may be the place God will reveal his glory to you and your loved ones. It may be the story you tell future generations.

Faith to Stop Looking Back

After Israel left Egypt, they spent forty years whining, wanting to return—to slavery! Israel's stubborn refusal to trust God did what Pharaoh's army and the Red Sea couldn't—kept them from the Promised Land. Wiersbe said, "It took but one night for God to take Israel out of Egypt, but it took forty years to take Egypt out of Israel."[18]

Our spiritual enemy tries to rob our present and future by luring us to look back. He makes what we left appear better than it was. Or he whispers, "The Lamb's blood is not enough. You'll never be free." We can't move forward while staring in the rearview mirror.

In contrast, Moses, who'd been a prince in Egypt, never looked back with longing. He had experienced the emptiness of worldly wealth and understood what Jesus meant when he later said, "Life does not consist in an abundance of possessions" (Luke 12:15).

Have you left the old life you knew before Christ? Like Moses, let's look forward, not back. The best is yet to be.

Moses's backstory helps us appreciate all God accomplished through him. God used Moses to deliver the Hebrews out of Egypt and give us the law. He became the mediator of the Old Covenant, as Jesus is the mediator of the New Covenant. The sufferings Moses endured were not worth comparing with the glory that followed (Rom. 8:18).

Since then, no prophet has risen in Israel like Moses, whom the LORD knew face to face, who did all those signs and wonders the LORD sent him to do in Egypt— to Pharaoh and to all his officials and to his whole land. For no one has ever shown the mighty power or performed the awesome deeds that Moses did in the sight of all Israel. (Deut. 34:10–12)

Today's Strength Builder

Is someone or something from your past (a loss or regret) hindering your walk with God? Leave your concerns with the Savior and move forward.

CLOSING PRAYER

Use this space to turn your insights and responses into prayers.

Prayer Requests

Strength to Follow God's Lead

JOSHUA AWOKE WITH A START. HIS MUFFLED CRY HALTED the nightmare—but not his fears. Perspiration drenched his body. He sat up and inhaled the crisp night air. He focused on his breathing and listened to the familiar night sounds. His racing heart slowed.

The nightmares began after Moses had passed the burden of leadership to him. The angry voices in his dream were shadows of the past. He knew how the scene would end. Worse, he couldn't stop the anarchy.

Lord, what if it happens again? If they wouldn't listen to Moses, why would they follow me? How do I know this time will be different?

Can you spot what's missing from this chronology of Israel's history? Israel—

- Left Egypt.
- Crossed the Red Sea.
- Marched around Jericho.

Because Hebrews 11 highlights faith, it completely skipped the forty years Israel spent wandering in the desert. Egypt represents the world. Israel left Egypt to go to the Promised Land to worship God. But fear waylaid her. She wandered forty years in a wilderness of unbelief.

Would the next generation choose faith and face the giants that stood between them and the Promised Land? The Bible says God "has blessed us with every spiritual blessing in the heavenly realms because we are united with Christ" (Eph. 1:3 NLT). Yet, like Israel, only those who walk by faith enjoy those blessings in this life. This week a Hebrew general and a pagan prostitute will show us how to follow God's lead and enjoy the riches of his grace.

Day One
Preparing for Victory

"Have I not commanded you? Be strong and coura-
geous. Do not be afraid; do not be discouraged, for
the LORD your God will be with you wherever you go."
—Joshua 1:9

Joshua means, "Jehovah is salvation."

In grade school, I balked when I had to miss recess because a few classmates provoked the teacher. But extra classwork didn't compare to the forty years Joshua and Caleb spent in the wilderness because their fellow Israelites disobeyed God.

Thirty-eight years before God called Joshua to lead the Israelites into Canaan, Israel rebelled against Moses and refused to enter the Promised Land. Joshua and Caleb had begged Israel not to cave into their fears. They'd pleaded with them to trust God. But Israel rebelled anyway.

The sweet taste of Canaan's fruit soured into bitter disappointment when Joshua couldn't persuade the people to follow God's lead. God bolted the door to the Promised Land on that rebellious generation. Joshua recalled that terrible day every time they buried someone from that group.

The time to lead the next generation into the Promised Land arrived. How would this group face the impenetrable walls of Jericho? The people promised to obey Joshua like they had obeyed Moses. When Moses had urged them to enter the land, they'd threatened to stone him!

On the other hand, were they ready to fight seasoned warriors? Even if they had chariots—which they didn't—how could they get past those city walls? What would keep his men from deserting in the middle of a battle?

Pondering Israel's past failures and current obstacles would intimidate any general. God saw Joshua's concerns and drew his focus to the source of his strength.

Entering Canaan, Not Heaven

Canaan (the Promised Land) depicts a life of faith—not heaven. In Canaan, the Israelites fought battles. They experienced blessings, growth, and defeat. Praise God. There are no battles or defeats in heaven. But, on earth, a life of faith includes both.

Did you get that? Battles don't mean you've done something wrong. Battles mean you're not home yet. We live on guard in enemy territory. Trouble lays surprise attacks.

When my husband and I toured Israel, I gained a fresh appreciation of what it means to live prepared. Our guide pointed across a span of land and said, "That's Jordan." Shifting his arm, he added, "And that's Syria. Israel's soldiers are always alert. We're either preparing for war or at war."

His words apply to life. Let's see how God prepared Joshua and how it relates to us.

Scripture Reading..

"By faith the walls of Jericho fell, after the army had marched around them for seven days." —Hebrews 11:30

JOSHUA 1:1–9

Study and Reflection

1. List the promises God gave Joshua (Josh. 1:1–5).

2. How do God's promises to Israel foreshadow his promises to us? See the following: "Praise be to the God and Father of our Lord Jesus Christ, who has blessed us in the heavenly realms with every spiritual blessing in Christ" (Eph. 1:3). "God has said, 'Never will I leave you; never will I forsake you.' So we say with confidence, 'The LORD is my helper; I will not be afraid. What can mere mortals do to me?'" (Heb. 13:5–6).

3. What did Joshua have to do to succeed on his mission (Josh. 1:6–9)?

4. The Book of the Law, or Instruction, refers to the first five books of the Bible written by Moses. It was the Bible of Joshua's day. God told Israel's new leader to meditate on that instruction day and night. Connect meditating on God's Word with Joshua's military success. Apply this to our modern lives. How does meditating on God's Word relate to success in marriage, parenting, business, and ministry?

5. Why do you think God repeated the message, "Be strong and very courageous"?

6. According to the following passage, what benefits come from meditating on Scripture? Which ones do you need today?

> The law of the LORD is perfect,
>   refreshing the soul.
> The statutes of the LORD are trustworthy,
>   making wise the simple.
> The precepts of the LORD are right,
>   giving joy to the heart.
> The commands of the LORD are radiant,
>   giving light to the eyes. . . .
> By them your servant is warned;
>   in keeping them there is great reward. (Ps. 19:7–8, 11)

7. Record any final thoughts or takeaways from today's lesson.

Meditate and Obey

A simple email punched me in the stomach. It looked like my hard work on a project had failed. At bedtime, the stone in my gut had not dissolved. I opened my Bible and sent up an arrow prayer, "Please speak to me."

I read, "The Israelites had traveled in the wilderness for forty years until all the men who were old enough to fight in battle when they left Egypt had died. For they had disobeyed the LORD, and the

LORD vowed he would not let them enter the land he had sworn to give us—a land flowing with milk and honey" (Josh. 5:6 NLT).

How, I wondered, does that speak to my issue? Then I recalled my morning meditation from Joshua 1:9 (NLT), "This is my command—be strong and courageous! Do not be afraid or discouraged. For the LORD your God is with you wherever you go."

God had commanded me not to be discouraged! To wallow in disappointment put me in the company of the disobedient Israelites and kept me from experiencing his blessings. I thought about the rest of the verse. God is with me. I smiled. God had given me better things to think about.

Why do we need to meditate on God's Word day and night? Because we are embroiled in a spiritual battle. The world, the flesh, and the devil bombard us twenty-four hours a day with defeating thoughts. God's Word is the sword that shreds our enemy's lies and exposes our distorted beliefs (Eph. 6:17; Heb. 4:12).

It's easy to chew on regrets, insults, defeats, and worries. But the Lord told Joshua to ruminate on his Word. The Bible refreshes us, makes us wise, and imparts joy and understanding. "In keeping [his commands] there is great reward" (Ps. 19:11).

Studying the Bible prepares us for life, like going over the plays of a sport prepares us for a game. The better we know God's words, the more naturally they flow. But to read the Bible and not apply it is like carrying a flashlight we never bother to turn on. We stumble through life like one groping in the dark. The Bible lights our way only when we use it.

The Lord said, "Study this Book of Instruction continually. Meditate on it day and night so you will be sure to obey everything written in it. Only then will you prosper and succeed in all you do" (Josh. 1:8 NLT). When we study, meditate, and apply, God's truth opens our eyes and prospers our souls.

Our personal choices, like links on a chain, impact our families, communities, and nation. Imagine dangling from a helicopter on a rusty chain. Your stomach turns when you look down from the dizzying height. Your chest tightens when you notice one of the links holding you pulling apart.

God's plan for nations requires individual obedience. In Joshua chapter 7, one man's sin caused Israel's military defeat and great loss. As a chain is only as strong as its weakest link, so my obedience matters to all of us. So does yours.

Today's Strength Builder

God told Joshua to meditate on his Word day and night. If the ten rebellious spies had meditated on what God had already accomplished, they would have entered the Promised Land forty years earlier. This week use Joshua 1:9 to "meditate, muse, and imagine."[1] Record what comes from this exercise.

CLOSING PRAYER

Use this space to turn your insights and responses into prayers.

Day Two

Active Faith

Rahab means "broad" or "wide."[2]

"I'm sending you on a secret mission." Joshua's dark eyes looked from one man to the other. "Scout out the land on the other side of the Jordan, especially Jericho."

The men nodded. They understood Joshua hoped to keep this mission undercover and avoid a repeat of the showdown Moses experienced. Joshua didn't need to confirm God's will. He needed eyes and ears inside the city.

The spies reached Jericho and slipped through the bustling city gates, hoping to blend in with the crowd. After a steady diet of manna, the baskets of dates and pomegranates, along with the pungent smell of spices, made their mouths water.

Feeling they were being watched, they ducked into an inn built into the city wall. The proximity to the city gate would provide a quick escape if needed. A young woman in colorful garb and kohl-rimmed eyes welcomed them and ushered them upstairs. They didn't question her in-charge manner. She led them to the rooftop terrace and pointed.

"Lie down," she said, grabbing the flax drying on her roof and swiftly covering them. "Stay put until I come for you."

Loud pounding and voices below made their hearts jump. The men had little choice but to trust her.

Today, we meet a special young woman. Rahab had never met a follower of Yahweh. She had little knowledge of the one true God, but she exercised the understanding she had. She reminds us faith isn't about how much we know but about what we do with what we know. Her bold faith secured her a place in four books of the Bible and in Jesus's family tree.

Scripture Reading..
JOSHUA 2:1–24

Study and Reflection

1. How did Rahab show she believed in God and his promise (Josh. 2:2–13)?

2. Someone recognized the spies and reported them to the king. A prostitute was the last person the spies expected to provide protection and demonstrate faith in their God. What do you draw from this unexpected story twist?

3. Remember when God allowed Israel to be caught between Pharaoh's army and the Red Sea? I wonder if God had Rahab and Joshua in mind when he orchestrated that event. Telling the stories of our experiences with our wonder-working God spreads seed. And we never know where that seed will take root and bear fruit. How did hearing about God's deliverance of Israel forty years earlier prepare the way for the Israelites (Josh. 2:10–11)?

4. Many seem to value religious experiences over simple faith. Witnessing the miraculous parting of the Red Sea certainly qualifies as a spectacular experience. But did it build faith? Most of the Israelites who witnessed God's miraculous deliverance later rebelled against him in unbelief. Yet Rahab, who only heard the story, risked her and her family's lives to follow God. What does this tell you about the power of

hearing God's stories? "So faith comes from hearing, that is, hearing the Good News about Christ" (Rom. 10:17 NLT).

5. What did Rahab have to do to be saved (Josh. 2:14, 17–20)?

6. Why do you think the Bible uses "prostitute" by Rahab's name when it commends her in the New Testament (Heb. 11:31)? "Rahab the prostitute is another example. She was shown to be right with God by her actions when she hid those messengers and sent them safely away by a different road" (James 2:25 NLT).

7. Record your final thoughts from today's lesson.

Faith, the Great Equalizer

Jericho was on high alert. Rahab's quick response to the spies makes me wonder if she'd prayed for an opportunity to know their God. For a woman to own an inn in a prime location for travelers suggests she had royal connections. Perhaps she had an arrangement with the king to report any chatter she overheard from travelers. In this case, however, instead of turning the Hebrews in for a fat bonus, she hid them in the hope of an eternal reward.

Hebrews highlights the faith of Rahab by name and Joshua by association. Compare their two profiles:

Rahab	Joshua
Ammonite (enemies of God)	Descendant of Abraham (chosen by God)
Pagan	Hebrew believer
Prostitute	Military general
Knowledge of God—hearsay	Eyewitness to God's miracles
Raised to worship pagan gods	Mentored by Moses
Courageous	Courageous
Commended for her faith	Faithful to God

While God held a special relationship with Israel, he "does not show favoritism but accepts from every nation the one who fears him and does what is right" (Acts 10:34–35). His grace includes lowly prostitutes and esteemed generals.

Forty years earlier, Israel experienced God's miraculous deliverance from Egypt. They followed the cloud by day and the pillar of fire by night. They plodded through the Red Sea and watched God close the water over Pharaoh's pursuing chariots. Yet they rebelled when God told them to enter the land he had promised them.

In contrast, God's stories revealed big problems for Rahab. God had promised to give her homeland to his people. Look at what his promises meant for Rahab and her people:

- The Hebrew God was more powerful than her god. He'd defeated Pharaoh, parted the Red Sea, and destroyed two powerful Ammonite kings.
- The Hebrew God was kinder than her god. While Jericho's god demanded the sacrifice of live babies, the Hebrew God fought for his people.
- The Hebrew God was holy. Rahab worked as a professional prostitute. Did a holy God even want someone like her?
- The Hebrew God had promised to bless his people by overthrowing her people!

Big Problems, No Problem for a Big God

Maybe when you first heard about God, like Rahab, you discovered you had some big problems. You'd spent your life serving the wrong gods—the gods of money, career, family, or education. Next to a holy God, you also came up short.

Jericho heard the stories about God, and their hearts melted in fear. Rahab heard the stories and declared, "The LORD your God is God in heaven above and on the earth below" (Josh. 2:11). The land belonged to God. It was his to give to Israel.

Hearing about the Red Sea miracle, which happened before she was born, so impacted this pagan prostitute that her life shifted 180 degrees to faith. Rahab discovered a God with the power and compassion to save her and her family.

Rahab demonstrates that what we do with our present opportunities matters more than a past we can't change. Little biblical knowledge is no excuse for disobeying God in what we do know. Rahab didn't have Moses's Book of Instruction. She held no prestigious position. However, she listened to the stories about Yahweh and obeyed his prompting to hide the spies and ask for kindness. God delighted in this young woman enough to place her in his own Son's genealogy (Matt. 1:5).

God wants to bring glory to his name in your challenges too. Your crisis might be another's salvation—or your own. What might he do with us if we practice bold faith?

Today's Strength Builder

Think about your faith story, whether it is how you came to know the Lord or a time he rescued you. Organize your thoughts and write out your story. Ask God for opportunities to share your Big God story.

CLOSING PRAYER
Use this space to turn your insights and responses into prayers.

Day Three
Do-Over

*"I—yes, I alone—will blot out your sins for my own
sake and will never think of them again."*
—Isaiah 43:25 (NLT)

Have you ever wished you could delete parts of your past? Push a computer key, and *poof*, your embarrassing moments disappear. Words said in anger—gone. Failures—erased.

Sometimes, God graciously provides do-overs. He did this for Israel when he had her repeat many actions they must have associated with their rebellion after escaping Egypt. This fresh start gave them the chance to tie these events to faith and success.

In my own life and in the lives of clients I've counseled, I've noticed God often allows new situations to tap old wounds and failures. God uses the current discomfort to help us face our past pain in his strength and find deliverance from old injuries. The next time an old wound unsettles you, consider it a gracious opportunity for a do-over.

Scripture Reading..

JOSHUA 3:1–17; 4:14–24; 5:1–12
"If I had not confessed the sin in my heart, the Lord would not have listened." —Psalm 66:18 (NLT)

MATTHEW 5:8

Study and Reflection

1. The ark of the covenant of the Lord was a chest that held the Ten Commandments, a gold jar of manna, and the rod of Aaron (Heb. 9:4). It represented God's presence. Israel was to follow the priests when they carried the ark into the Promised Land (Josh. 3:1–6, 11). What spiritual application do you draw from this?

2. To prepare for crossing the Jordan, Joshua told the people to "consecrate, sanctify, prepare, dedicate, be hallowed, be holy, be sanctified, be separate,"[3] "for tomorrow the LORD will do amazing things among you" (Josh. 3:5). How does personal purity affect someone's ability to experience God (Matt. 5:8; Ps. 66:18)?

3. According to Joshua 3:7, what would make Joshua a great leader in the eyes of the people?

4. Think of the different authority figures whose decisions affect you in or at home, work, church, the community, and the world. What difference does knowing a leader follows the Lord make to you?

5. What miracle did God perform for Israel that echoed what he'd done for Moses (Josh. 3:12–17; 4:23)?

6. How did God keep his promise to Joshua (Josh. 4:14)?

7. Name two reasons why God dried up the riverbed
   (Josh. 4:23–24).

8. "Today I have rolled away the reproach of Egypt from you"
   (Josh. 5:9). Some see this as the disgrace of having been
   slaves—a role imposed on them. Others see this as the shame
   of refusing to enter the Promised Land and wanting to return
   to Egypt forty years earlier. After long years of manna and
   wilderness, the Lord led Israel through purification, crossing the Jordan, and circumcision. They celebrated Passover
   together. The following day, the manna stopped, and they ate
   produce from Canaan. What lessons and encouragement do
   you take from this?

9. Record any final thoughts from today's lesson.

Your Do-Over

"Their sins and lawless acts I will remember no more." —Hebrews 10:17

A scene in C. S. Lewis's *The Silver Chair* captures Christ's desire to
restore us after we've failed. Jill faces the great lion Aslan after she
messed up her assignment:

> [Jill] remembered only how she had made Eustace fall
> over the cliff, and how she had helped to muff nearly all
> the signs, and about all the snappings and quarrellings.

And she wanted to say "I'm sorry," but she could not speak. Then the Lion drew them towards him with his eyes, and bent down and touched their pale faces with his tongue, and said, "Think of that no more. I will not always be scolding. You have done the work for which I sent you into Narnia."[4]

Like Jill, Israel muffed their assignment. But God gave them a fresh start that began with purification. Jesus offers to cleanse us when we mess up too. "If we confess our sins, he is faithful and just and will forgive us our sins and purify us from all unrighteousness" (1 John 1:9). God removes our shame, whether from something done to us or by us.

Our word "confess" comes from the Greek word "*homologeō*," which means "to say the same thing" or "to agree with."[5] When we confess our sins, we agree with what God says about our sins. Confession demonstrates faith that Jesus's blood is sufficient to cover our sins and restore fellowship with him. When we confess our sins, we align our wills and values with his. We agree his views are right, and we agree Jesus paid for every sin we've committed or ever will commit.

Sometimes I've felt worse over my mistakes than my sins. How could I have not seen how this would play out? I knew Jesus had taken care of my sins, but I felt I had to pay for my mistakes.

We're not omniscient. Hindsight has knowledge foresight lacks. The only fatal mistake is to reject Jesus. If God is big enough to handle the sin that affects our eternity, he's big enough to cover errors in judgment.

If you're carrying shame or regret, let Jesus take that for you. "Come to me, all you who are weary and burdened, and I will give you rest" (Matt. 11:28).

Dwelling on sin and mistakes creates distance in our relationship with the Lord. Confess your failures and accept his cleansing. Celebrate your Passover Lamb. We join Israel in unbelief when we question whether his blood is sufficient to cover all our sins and mistakes.

Remember his invitation: "'Come now, let us settle the matter,' says the LORD. 'Though your sins are like scarlet, they shall be as white as snow'" (Isa. 1:18).

In Israel's do-over, God reminded them of his unchanging character and power. Is it easier to conquer an enemy, personal sin, or a force of nature like a river at flood stage? The Lord dried up the Jordan to show he has power over all three. Fear of God would protect Israel from sin, human enemies, and the forces of nature.

> The LORD your God did to the Jordan what he had
> done to the Red Sea when he dried it up before us until
> we had crossed over. He did this so that all the peoples
> of the earth might know that the hand of the LORD is
> powerful and so that you might always fear the LORD
> your God. (Josh. 4:23–24)

Today's Strength Builder

Do you need a do-over? Ask the Holy Spirit to point out any area that needs healing, cleansing, or refreshing. Write it down and use a prayer like the one under Closing Prayer to experience cleansing. Then write 1 John 1:9 across the words. Shred the paper and begin clean again.

CLOSING PRAYER

Use this space to turn your insights and responses into prayers. Here is a suggested prayer to release any regret and guilt.

Lord Jesus, I'm very sorry I _____ (tell him what you did or didn't do). Thank you for forgiving and cleansing me from all unrighteousness. Empower me to live a life that pleases you.

Day Four
Who's in Charge?

I brought home seasonal vegetables to roast for a fall meal. My daughter saw them and pictured an Asian stir-fry. She ran to the grocery store to get the ingredients for the sauce and extra veggies to add to mine.

Trying to be helpful, she told me how to slice the vegetables. I didn't like the way she washed the mushrooms and rewashed them. She piled an extra layer of veggies over the pan I had ready to roast. Having two head chefs was not working. Finally, I said, "How about I roast these veggies the way I planned, and you use the ones you got with your sauce? We'll have two dishes instead of one big one." She agreed. Once we knew our roles, we prepared the meal in harmony.

Have you ever tried to work on a project with two people leading in different directions? Someone needs to be in charge. Today we see someone is. When we follow his lead, our churches, families, businesses, and lives fall into place.

Scripture Reading..
JOSHUA 5:13–6:5

Study and Reflection

1. "Now when Joshua was near Jericho, he looked up and saw a man standing in front of him with a drawn sword in his hand. Joshua went up to him and asked, 'Are you for us or for our enemies?'" (Josh. 5:13). What does the warrior's answer reveal about his loyalties (Josh. 5:14)? How do you apply this to how we should live?

2. Many commentators believe the commander of the Lord's army was the preincarnate Christ. This manifestation is called a Christophany. Joshua's actions support this. How do the commander's words echo Moses's experience at the burning bush (Exod. 3:5; Josh. 5:15)? What does Joshua's response teach us about faith?

3. Do you think Joshua welcomed being second-in-command under the captain of the Lord's army? Why or why not? How does Joshua's experience with the captain of the Lord's army relate to us? "God has put all things under the authority of Christ and has made him head over all things for the benefit of the church" (Eph. 1:22 NLT).

4. What do you learn about the first city Israel had to face in Canaan that could have unnerved them (Josh. 6:1)?

5. Seven is God's number for completeness and perfection. Why was faith necessary to execute the battle plan the Lord gave Joshua?

6. Record any final thoughts or takeaways from today's lesson.

The Joy of Knowing Who's in Charge

Before Joshua faced Jericho, the Lord met with him in a manner similar to his meeting with Moses. He appeared in the burning bush to the shepherd Moses and as a warrior to General Joshua. These encounters were similar enough to show the Lord does not change but different enough to show God treats us as individuals. God speaks in distinct ways we understand.

The Lord said to Joshua, "See, I've delivered Jericho into your hands." No, Joshua probably didn't *see* how marching around Jericho once a day for six days and seven times on the seventh day would conquer this fortified city. Once he knew the orders came from God, Joshua had no trouble bowing to plans that defied human reason. God had chosen Joshua to lead Israel, but the captain of the Lord's army was in charge. Joshua would gladly follow him.

Joshua didn't know how Israel could penetrate Jericho's walls, walls deep enough for two chariots to ride side by side on top of the wall. He didn't need to understand how God would use trumpets and marching to destroy a city. He needed only to follow God's instructions.

It's not up to us to figure out how to conquer our challenges either. God says, "Trust in the LORD with all your heart and lean not on your own understanding; in all your ways submit to him, and he will make your paths straight" (Prov. 3:5–6). As we submit to God's known will—even when it seems counterintuitive—he directs our steps and accomplishes what concerns us.

Like Joshua, we identify the leader. The Holy Spirit never contradicts God's Word, but he may challenge our understanding and application of his Word. Joshua's soldiers didn't take a Sabbath rest in the middle of battle. Godly counsel can help us discern God's voice. However, realize that sometimes respected Christians won't always agree. Make sure the advice you follow encourages you to seek the Lord's voice. As we pursue his will, he guides us. His will trumps human opinion, regardless of the human.

We live in a culture that blurs the line between right and wrong. Many believe they know best and don't need an antiquated book to guide them. The Bible warns, "There is a way that appears to be right, but in the end it leads to death" (Prov. 14:12).

One of Joshua's soldiers thought he could stretch the Lord's limits at Jericho (Josh. 7). Achan hid one of the forbidden articles for himself. His defiance cost Israel her next battle and brought death to thirty-six Israelite soldiers, himself, and his family. God's limits protect us. Those who violate them, like drunk drivers, harm innocent people as well as themselves.

Joshua didn't tell the Lord how much time they'd save if they cut the number of days circling Jericho from seven to three. We don't need to waste energy squabbling about God's ways and timetable either. We may not understand why his ways work, but faith follows the leader. Changes in the culture don't alter God or his decrees.

Those who demand the rationale for God's ways before they'll trust and obey live defeated. As a young believer, I tried to understand how God can be sovereign and yet hold humans responsible for their choices. How could he be just and allow some people to receive better starts in life? Finally, I realized my wrestling over what I couldn't understand was going nowhere. My joy returned when I humbly acknowledged I didn't need to understand to trust and obey (Deut. 29:29). As Paul wrote, "Oh, the depth of the riches of the wisdom and knowledge of God! How unsearchable his judgments, and his paths beyond tracing out!" (Rom. 11:33).

How can we, stained by sin, judge the one who is holy, holy, holy? How can our selfish natures comprehend selfless love? God is love; he alone has the right to define love (1 John 4:8). He outlines right and wrong because he alone is righteous. He knows the consequences each choice brings (Prov. 8:36). We can trust him.

Joshua didn't need to understand how marching around Jericho would defeat their enemy or why they had to be quiet until the final shout. He needed to direct his troops to obey. Reverence, not understanding, guided his steps. His obedience brought victory.

When we know who's in charge, we can relax. We don't quit thinking, but we don't waste energy challenging God's revealed will.

Feeling overwhelmed or responsible may indicate a need to recall who's in charge. Our Captain accomplishes what concerns us. Let's follow his lead.

Today's Strength Builder

What are you wrestling over? Take your questions to Jesus. Seek his instructions. Relinquish control and let him lead.

CLOSING PRAYER

Use this space to turn your insights and responses into prayers.

Day Five

Faith Is Not in a Hurry—Trusting God's Timing

Patience is not my strong suit. Sometimes my hurrying doesn't make sense even to me. I want to check something off my list and move on. To what? Why am I in a rush? I couldn't tell you.

God is patient. But his waits are never arbitrary. He's at work, even when we can't see it.

The Lord told Abraham the sin of the Amorites was not yet complete (Gen. 15:16). He would wait for their sin to fully ripen before executing judgment. During the 440-year wait, Jericho, an Amorite nation, received enough knowledge to repent of wickedness. Israel marched around Jericho for seven days, providing one more week for Jericho to call out to God before judgment fell. Yet only Rahab repented and trusted God. Only Rahab's family joined her and was saved.

The Bible calls Jericho's refusal to surrender to God "disobedience" (Heb. 11:31). They knew judgment was coming. Yet, unlike Rahab, they refused to bow before the Lord and ask for mercy. Biblical faith is more a matter of the will than the mind and emotions (Acts 28:26–27; James 2:19; Heb. 3:15–19).

Was the wait profitable? Read Rahab's story and decide.

Scripture Reading...

"It was by faith that the people of Israel marched around Jericho for seven days, and the walls came crashing down. It was by faith that Rahab the prostitute was not destroyed with the people in her city who refused to obey God. For she had given a friendly welcome to the spies." —Hebrews 11:30-31 (NLT)

JOSHUA 6:6–27

Study and Reflection

1. Record your observations on this exciting story.

2. What spiritual lessons do you see in this passage?

3. How do they apply to you?

4. The generation that walked through the Red Sea and lived through the ten plagues had every reason to trust God's power. Yet, compared to their enemy, they felt like grasshoppers (Num. 13:33). They rebelled against Moses and God and refused to enter Canaan. Four decades later, Israel defeated Jericho, but not because of military power. What do you learn from this?

5. Who from Jericho survived this battle (Josh. 6:22–25)?

6. Record any final takeaways from today's lesson.

What a Prostitute and a General Teach Us about Faith

Rahab and her family jostled to view the soldiers marching around their city. She counted seven men blowing trumpets. Otherwise, no one spoke. Her spine tingled when a couple of the soldiers eyed the red cord hanging from her window.

When would they attack? What were they waiting for?

For six days, the men came, circled the city, and left. The seventh day began like the previous six, but this time they continued to circle—two, three . . . seven times. When would they strike?

Loud trumpet blasts and thunderous shouts made Rahab jump. Her walls shook. Neighbors screamed. Dust stung her nose and eyes. What was happening? How could the spies save her if she lay buried under Jericho's walls?

Her family bolted for the door, but Rahab was quicker. "No!" she shouted above the clamor, spreading her arms to bar the exit. "We must stay put."

Faith in Action

The spies didn't know the walls would collapse when they told Rahab to gather her family inside her home and hang the scarlet cord outside her window. The captain of the Lord's army hadn't yet given General Joshua those battle plans. If they had known, surely, they wouldn't have told her to stay in her house while the walls crumbled. Had they messed up?

Rahab heard the good news about God, responded to his prompting to hide the Hebrew spies, and followed their directions from start to finish. As Israel had put lamb's blood on their doors, Rahab hung the scarlet cord out of her window as a sign of her trust in Yahweh. And death passed her by.

Rabbi Jonathan Cahn writes, "The Gospel must *always* lead to Acts. You see, it's not enough to hear the Gospel message. It must produce change. You must act on it."[6]

It didn't matter that the spies didn't know God's plan. Nor did it matter that the wall that supported Rahab's house would disintegrate. What mattered was she trusted the Lord. He was her hiding place and saved her from destruction. Her name lives on as an ancestor of Jesus and an example of faith and God's grace.

Rahab's courageous faith moved her to transfer her allegiance from the king of Jericho to the King of heaven. It directed her to hide the spies. Her contagious faith strengthened her to stay planted when every instinct told her to flee her quaking house.

The Amorites had become so wicked that they sacrificed their own children. Perhaps God waited all those years to destroy Jericho so he could save Rahab and her family and add her bloodline to his Son's family tree.

Joshua demonstrated faith by having his men march around Jericho day after day, even when they could not see how their marching made a difference. Marching seven times as long on the day they would fight didn't seem logical. But they obeyed. And God dropped the walls in an instant.

Sometimes we pray and pray, and nothing happens. At times God calls us to stay planted when our instincts shout, "Flee!" This story reminds us not to put our faith in what we see but to trust the invisible God who commanded us to persevere in prayer and obedience. I'm sure, after the victory, the Hebrews recognized how much better God's plan was than their butting a log against the gates. Let's not beat our heads against God's plan. We may be one lap away from seeing the walls crumble.

Today's Strength Builder

Waiting is often a necessary part of our development. Psalm 32:8 says, "I will instruct you and teach you in the way you should go;

I will counsel you with my loving eye on you." What does that mean for you today?

CLOSING PRAYER

Use this space to turn your insights and responses into prayers.

Prayer Requests

Strength for Shaky Faith

Gideon means "hewer; he who strikes down."

"My power is made perfect in weakness."
—2 Corinthians 12:9

GIDEON MOPPED HIS SWEATY BROW. IF ONLY A WET CLOTH could cool his anger.

"The Lord is with you, mighty warrior."

Gideon whirled to see who'd spoken. Was the stranger mocking him? And that bit about the Lord being with him . . . Gideon swallowed his cynicism. "Sir, if the Lord is with us, why has this happened? Where are the miracles? The Lord who brought our ancestors out of Egypt has abandoned us."

"Go and rescue Israel from the Midianites," the angel of the Lord said. "I am sending you!"

Doubts swirled inside of Gideon like thrashed chaff. "Me? My clan is the weakest in Manasseh, and I . . . I'm the least in my family."

"I'll be with you," the Lord said. "You will destroy the Midianites as if you were fighting one man."

Gideon pressed his fingers into his forehead, hoping to make sense of these words. "Sir, if you really are the Lord, please, give me a sign."

Many associate Gideon with his famous fleeces. Did you realize those fleeces showed weakness, not strength? It took an encounter with the angel of the Lord, two fleeces, and a dream to prop up Gideon's weak faith. But Gideon's strength grew with each exchange. His growth began when he asked for help to believe.

Has God placed a dream in your heart? A wrong to right? A cause to champion? Or a child to train? What fear keeps you in hiding? Perhaps God has impressed a neighbor on your heart or a ministry to join, but you feel inadequate for these assignments.

Gideon carried a burden to rescue his people. Someone needed to do something, but who was he to step up? Could one person make a difference?

Maybe you're asking yourself, "Who am I to step up?" Ask God to speak to you today. The one who assured Gideon can do the same for you.

Day One
Discovering the Root of the Problem

My children knew our house rules. We don't put shoes on furniture or yell indoors. We dedicate Sunday mornings to church. What the neighborhood kids did in their homes was their parents' business.

The children of Israel knew their heavenly Father's rules too. They knew the special favor God bestowed on Abraham and his descendants. They knew how he'd delivered their ancestors from Pharaoh, parted the Red Sea and the Jordan River, provided manna to feed them for forty years in the desert, and kept their shoes and clothing from wearing out. They understood the blessings that came from heeding the Ten Commandments and the curses that came from turning a deaf ear. Yet, as a nation, they ignored the laws, beginning with the first commandment: "You shall have no other gods before me" (Exod. 20:3).

Despite a long and miraculous history, Israel did evil in God's sight and put other gods before him. They mixed idolatry with the worship of God and created an adulterated belief system that removed the covering of Jehovah's protective wings (Ps. 91).

Before introducing Gideon, Judges 6 explains the circumstances in which Gideon lived. God even sent Israel a prophet explaining the reason for her misery. The Bible describes the period of the Judges as a time when "all the people did whatever seemed right in their own eyes" (Judg. 17:6 NLT).

Like the good father with his prodigal son in Luke 15:11–32, God allowed the Israelites to choose their path and experience the consequences of their choices. When they tired of life in the pig pen and came to their senses, they would come home. When they did, he provided a deliverer. This time, God tapped Gideon.

Scripture Reading..
JUDGES 6:1–10
"Godliness makes a nation great, but sin is a disgrace to any people."
—Proverbs 14:34 (NLT)

Study and Reflection

1. Why was Israel oppressed (Judg. 6:1)?

2. Israel didn't stand out as worse than the surrounding nations. But, unlike her neighbors, God's chosen people knew better (Deut. 29:16–18). To have enjoyed God's favor, provision, and

protection and then reject him made her sins doubly evil in God's eyes. We live in a rapidly changing culture that openly applauds what the Bible calls sin. Why does a nation's morality matter (Prov. 14:34)?

3. Sin is never isolated. When an individual, a family, or a nation walks away from God, they leave his umbrella of protection. The innocent suffer along with the guilty. How did Israel suffer?

4. What caused Israel to finally call out to the Lord (Judg. 6:6)?

5. Israel thought their problem was the Midianites. When they cried out because of Midian, God sent them a prophet (Judg. 6:7–10). Do you think Israel connected her suffering with her sin? Why was it important for Israel to recognize the real source of her problems?

6. Are you in the middle of some sort of misery? Have you asked God to help you? It hurts to discover we played a role in causing our unhappiness. But if that's true, we also have the power to impact positive change (Gal. 6:7–9). Ask God if there's any hurtful way in you that needs to change (Ps. 139:23–24). Sometimes, pain in one area is rooted in a different area. And national deliverance begins with personal repentance.

7. Record your final thoughts from today's lesson.

Why Am I Depressed?

Gloom choked the air like diesel exhaust at a bus stop. I plopped on the side of my bed and asked myself why. Two healthy preschoolers, a loving husband, a comfortable home, and a fruitful ministry should have added up to a satisfying life. Why, with so much good in my life, did I feel down?

Immediately, I sensed the answer.

You don't think I love you.

Dumbfounded, I knew it was true. According to my plans, I should have been finishing my master's degree in Biblical Studies. Instead, because of short finances, while our ministry team scattered for summer mission projects, we canceled our plans and stayed home.

Ironically, when the Holy Spirit uncovered my wrong belief, I felt relief. I knew God loved me. My spirit lifted despite my disappointing circumstances.

The Midianites descended from Abraham and Keturah (Gen. 25:1–2). At harvest time, they swooped into Israel like swarms of locusts to ravage Israel's crops.

But Midian wasn't the primary source of Israel's misery. The root of their suffering lay in Israel's idolatry, not their horrible circumstances. Gideon was wrong; God hadn't abandoned Israel. Israel had forsaken God.

While the Hebrews blamed others, they remained victims. But if Israel took responsibility for her actions and realigned herself with God, everything else would change too.

Knowing God is with us—even when we're suffering from our own making—strengthens us to face our fears, errors, and disappointments. Before we can change what's happening on the outside, we sometimes need God's transformation on the inside.

Today's Strength Builder

Have you felt forgotten by God? Ask him to show you the root of your problem. Could it be you've pinned your hope—or blame—in the wrong place?

CLOSING PRAYER

Use this space to turn your insights and responses into prayers.

Day Two
Drawing Out What God Put In

During his sermon, a preacher asked a woman to stand. "Do you trust me?"

"Yes, sir," she said.

"Will you do what I ask?"

"Yes," she nodded.

"Open your Bible and give me the $100 bill inside," he said.

She frowned. "I don't have a hundred dollars."

"Didn't you say you'd do what I asked? Please open your Bible and bring me the $100 bill."

She looked down at her Bible and hesitated, then flipped it open and gasped. There was a $100 bill. "How did you know?"

"I put it there to demonstrate that God always puts in us what he asks of us."

———

"You will not grow without attempting to do things you cannot do."
—Dr. Henry Cloud

Maybe, like Gideon, you're confronting a daunting challenge—an illness, a rebellious child, a broken relationship, or a spiraling career or bank account. You've done the math, and you come up short—short of energy, resources, and courage. But have you added Jesus to your equation?

Scripture says, "The eyes of the LORD search the whole earth in order to strengthen those whose hearts are fully committed to him" (2 Chron. 16:9 NLT). The Lord searched Israel and spotted an available heart buried under Gideon's frustration. The Lord didn't expect Gideon to defeat the Midianites in his own strength. Gideon just needed to trust and obey.

God partners with ordinary people to accomplish his will. When the Lord burdens our hearts with tasks too big for us, we can be sure he doesn't expect us to accomplish them alone. He expects us to follow his lead. We show up, and he shines. Showing up may be the hardest part of the battle.

Scripture Reading..
JUDGES 6:11–24
PHILIPPIANS 1:6; 2:13

Study and Reflection

1. The Lord appeared to Gideon when he was threshing wheat in a winepress. In normal circumstances, farmers used oxen to crush the grain and separated the worthless chaff in an open-air threshing floor on top of a hill where the wind could blow away the chaff released by threshing. Winepresses

were usually located at the bottom of a hill, sheltered away from the wind. Threshing in a winepress doubled Gideon's work and frustration. Walvoord and Zuck say, "Threshing wheat in a winepress reflected both his fear of discovery by the Midianites and the smallness of his harvest."[1] Contrast the angel of the Lord's greeting with Gideon's view of himself (Judg. 6:11–16).

2. Romans describes God as "the God who . . . calls into being things that were not" (Rom. 4:17). God called Abraham the father of many nations *before* Isaac was born. He called Gideon a mighty warrior while he was hiding. Gideon carried concern for his people before the Lord commissioned him (Judg. 6:13), but he lacked experience and strength. In each case, what God predicted came true. How do you apply this to yourself (Phil. 1:6, 2:13)?

3. Ephesians 2:10 says, "For we are God's handiwork, created in Christ Jesus to do good works, which God prepared in advance for us to do." Have you minimized a strength others notice? God equipped you to succeed in the work he planned for you. This is not the same as believing anyone can be anything they want. I'd like to sing like Celine Dion, but don't hold your breath. The angel told Gideon, "Go in the strength you have and save Israel out of Midian's hand. Am I not sending you?" What strength did Gideon have, according to Judges 6:16?

4. The Bible says, "Do not scoff at prophecies, but test everything that is said. Hold on to what is good" (1 Thess. 5:20–21
   NLT). Since not all prophetic words are God-inspired, we
   check them and any internal promptings against God's Word
   and character (Gal. 1:8). He won't lead us to do something
   that contradicts what he's already written. How did Gideon
   do this (Judg. 6:17–23)?

5. Consider the state in which the angel of the Lord found
   Gideon. What significance do you draw from the name
   Gideon called the altar (Judg. 6:24)?

6. Record any final thoughts or takeaways from today's lesson.

Are You Sure?

Every morning when I snuggled into my favorite chair to read
my Bible, the same thought marched across my mind. *Someone
needs to host a conference for our area youth.* "Lord, please raise
someone up," I prayed.

Finally, the pressure moved me to meet with our church youth
pastor. I presented the conference idea to him. He jumped on board.
"You can use our church. I'll support you in every way I can."

"Whoa, I don't want to lead. I thought you could do that. I know
a great speaker. And I'm happy to help."

"You lead it. I'm 100 percent behind you," he assured.

I reached out to another man I thought might take the reins.
After all, he ran youth programs at our local YMCA.

"Count me in," he said. But, like my youth pastor, he wanted me to spearhead it.

"God, do you want me to lead this?" The support of a prominent church and the local Y had come so easily. I was comfortable sharing the idea, but leading a multichurch conference?

As I prayed, individuals came to mind. Each one I approached jumped on board. God put together a team of major league players. One conference became two—one for teachers and parents and another for teens. Ministry friends from other states traveled to lead worship and teach.

God did immeasurably more than I could have hoped or imagined. The conference ended on my birthday. I listened for over an hour as students lined up to share how God had met them that weekend. Some smashed their anti-Christian music CDs. Others publicly asked forgiveness from other youth in their church groups. Still others found Christ for the first time. The best birthday gift ever! Decades later, people are still enjoying the transformation that began over those weekends.

However, this event was not without challenges:

- A car smashed into our prayer chair's car, cracking her spine.
- On the way to copy conference materials, my husband obeyed an internal warning to stay put when his traffic light turned green. Seconds later, a car sped through the intersection where he would have been.
- The four houses at the end of our cul-de-sac lost power on the morning of the parent conference. I showered at a friend's house. In an ironic twist, on the Saturday of the teen conference, a student rammed a light pole at the SAT test site knocking out their electricity, making it possible for several students to join our conference on time.

- The night before the teen conference, our keyboard player smashed his hand. God provided a gifted replacement who seamlessly followed the song leader without rehearsal or music.

Don't be dismayed if God leads you into battle. For, like the believers of old, we become strong in battle. Having a front-row seat of God in action is worth any inconvenience. As one friend who suffered COVID after a mission trip said, "Everyone who went on this trip and got COVID has said if they'd known they'd get COVID by going, they'd do it again to experience what we did."

God's strength needs our *yes* to be released. When the angel of the Lord tapped Gideon, God had a plan. Gideon compared himself with his enemy and questioned God's logic. How could the youngest member of the weakest clan deliver Israel from such a mighty army? Was this really the Lord speaking?

Gideon needed reassurance. The angel touched Gideon's offering with the tip of his staff. Fire flared from the rock and consumed his offering, and the angel vanished. Gideon recoiled in alarm.

He'd seen the angel of God face-to-face! Would he die? The angel assured him he wouldn't die. Gideon built an altar to the Lord and called it Jehovah-Shalom, "The Lord is Peace." The God of peace had heard Israel's cry. Gideon's circumstances hadn't changed. In fact, they would get worse before they got better. But encountering the Lord began a change in Gideon. Meeting the God of peace provided Gideon with the peace of God and the hope that, with God, he would become a mighty warrior.

How about you? What would be the greater miracle, to see your circumstances change or to experience God's peace in any circumstance? Believe you are who God says you are and align yourself with him.

Today's Strength Builder

God's presence, not Gideon's strength, determined the outcome of the battle against Midian. Gideon's role was to go forth believing God. Zechariah 4:6 describes *the strength we have*: "This is the word of the LORD to Zerubbabel: 'Not by might nor by power, but by my Spirit,' says the LORD Almighty." Go forth in God's strength today.

CLOSING PRAYER

Use this space to turn your insights and responses into prayers.

Lord Jesus, I believe. Help my unbelief.

Day Three
First Things First

Weren't the Midianites Israel's most pressing problem? Gideon thought so *before* his encounter with the angel of the Lord. After experiencing the Lord, he realized Israel's relationship with God came first.

Our relationship with God is the axis upon which life turns. Problems with our spouse, our children, or at work remind us to check our vertical relationship. When that relationship is off, everything else goes off-kilter too. Nothing satisfies. Life is either too hot or too cold—never just right. When our vertical relationship is right, we experience the peace of God even before we see improvement in other areas.

The armies of Midian and the other eastern peoples posed a real threat. But meeting the Lord clarified Gideon's vision. Tearing down his family's idols came before addressing the national threat. Doing so transformed Gideon in ways I don't think he could have imagined. In a sense, he held up a banner to his clan that said, "I serve Jehovah." His courage may have awakened his father's faith.

I identify with Gideon in many ways. I grew up in the church and knew the Lord but didn't learn to walk with him until college. When I sensed a call into full-time Christian work, I resisted. Surely our perfect God had made his first mistake. After wrestling with God, I surrendered and joined the staff of an international youth ministry where I was responsible for raising my financial support.

My family considered religion private. I recalled my youth group's incredulous response to a visitor who believed the Bible's stories. When my minister asked me to speak on Sunday morning and share what I'd be doing, my sister told me my peers were joking about "Debbie's conversion."

My knees quivered like Jell-O® as I climbed the steps to the ornate pulpit. However, God rewarded my obedience. Proclaiming what Jesus had done for me strengthened me in ways I would never have predicted. It tore down the idol of needing my peers' approval and opened the floodgates of God's favor.

The following week my church rallied around me. People who'd turned me down for ministry support asked to join my financial support team. In three days, God raised more funds than I had in the previous three months. I left that Friday for my New England assignment, having raised half of my yearly support in one week.

Before God uses us to further his kingdom, he may call us to smash our idols. Doing so is the first step to supernatural power and strength. Most of us don't display carved idols in our homes. What are our idols? An idol is anything that usurps God's rightful place in our lives. Be it a substance, relationship, habit, or job. We identify idols by how precious they are to us and the control they exert over us. Like Gideon's town and family, the flesh fights anyone—including people we love—who tries to remove this illegitimate source of security, significance, and well-being. Worshiping the true God frees us from their destructive hold (Judg. 6:26).

Scripture Reading..
JUDGES 6:25–40

Study and Reflection

1. After the angel of the Lord made his identity clear, what did Gideon have the faith to do (Judg. 6:25–27)?

2. That night, God asked Gideon to tear down his father's idols. Why did carrying out the Lord's command take faith and courage (Judg. 6:27b–32)?

3. Baal was the supreme male divinity of the Phoenicians or Canaanites.[2] An Asherah was a wooden pole representing a female deity and companion of Baal. Gideon's neighbors, who were part of God's chosen people, sought to kill Gideon, a fellow Israelite, after he smashed the forbidden idols (Judg. 6:28–30). We may not erect idols in our homes, but anger against anyone who suggests we give up a habit, a substance, or a relationship may indicate we've become ensnared in a form of idolatry. What warning do you take from this?

4. Some people say when they made a concerted effort to live for God, their circumstances got worse. After Gideon tore down his father's pagan altar, what did Israel's enemy do (Judg. 6:33)?

5. How did Gideon respond, and what prompted this action (Judg. 6:34–35)?[3]

6. After Gideon sounded the alarm to call Israel to war, do you think he had second thoughts? What do Gideon's two fleeces reveal about Gideon and his faith (Judg. 6:36–40)?

7. Record your final thoughts from today's lesson.

Seeking God or Seeking Assurance

Wouldn't it be nice if God told you exactly what he wanted you to do? Imagine entering university, certain you were in his perfect will. Starting a job knowing God had called you there for the next ten years. Knowing exactly who to marry and where to invest your retirement funds.

Do we imagine that receiving specific direction from the Lord will remove the need to trust? Biblical characters and my own experience show that, often, a clear call raises more questions. God's call can also tap our insecurities.

Gideon's assignment brought him face-to-face with his fears, doubts, and personal inadequacies. Gideon didn't ask for a fleece to discern God's will. He knew God had called him to fight (Judg. 6:14) and had promised victory. He wanted assurance God would keep his promise. The fleece showed doubt, not faith. "If you will save Israel by my hand *as you have promised—*"

In essence, Gideon was saying, "I know what you said. Will you keep your promise?"

Gideon's need for repeated assurance didn't put God off. Given the idolatrous practices of Gideon's tribe, God understood Gideon's misgivings and met his terms. God even provided additional encouragement before the great battle.

When we want to follow God, he moves Jupiter and Mars to help us. He isn't surprised when situations deflate our hope.

What biblical promise are you doubting? Don't be afraid to bring God your doubts. He wants your trust and success. Be honest with him and let him turn your weakness into strength.

Today's Strength Builder

What place does God hold in your life and family? What practical next step must you take to make or keep him first?

CLOSING PRAYER

Use this space to turn your insights and responses into prayers.

Day Four

From Weakness Made Strong

It's not the size of your enemy but the size of your God.

When problems camp out in our backyards like Gideon's Midianites—problems like learning your spouse is an addict, and he's emptied your savings account; or your doctor can't help your child, and you'll spend the rest of your life as her caretaker—we hope our troubles will disappear while we hide in our work. Like Gideon, we believe the challenge is too big.

Unfortunately, hiding doesn't work. We must face our challenges in God's strength, one day at a time. Sometimes, one minute at a time. When we do, we experience something better than magic. We experience God. We experience transformation.

Over lunch, my friend stunned me when she said she was thankful her husband had left her. While grateful he has since returned, she realizes his painful absence forced her to become rooted and grounded in God's love.

"I'm convinced my children are the people they are today because of what they saw take place in me during that agonizing time."

Gideon's challenges forced him to face his doubts and admit, "Lord, I know what you said. But can I trust you?"

I think it thrilled God to reassure Gideon. Per his request, God left the lamb's fleece wet and the floor dry. Gideon must have wondered if that was too easy. He asked for another sign. "This time, let the fleece be dry and the floor wet."

No problem. God did as Gideon asked.

Gideon didn't have our Bible. His family worshiped idols. Asking God for assurance showed he believed God existed and would reward his seeking (Heb. 11:6). By admitting his need for reassurance, Gideon learned Yahweh cared not only for Israel, the nation, he also cared for Gideon, the individual. Yahweh-Shalom became Gideon's peace even as the enemy gathered in force.

Challenging Our Perception

We may not live with an Asherah pole and altar to Baal, but our culture and experiences distort our perception of God, ourselves, and our circumstances. Those who grew up under the protection of a loving earthly father usually find it easier to emotionally rely on their heavenly Father. Those with emotionally or physically distant fathers may find it harder to trust God.

This principle hit home early in my counseling career when I listened to a young woman in ministry who was being transferred to a new area. When she explained her situation, I assumed she worried about not having adequate income for the move. In her shoes, that would have been my concern.

I grew up feeling close to my father but with a scarcity mind-set when it came to money. Daddy's father died when he was two. Growing up in a single-parent home during the depression taught him to be extremely frugal. After Mama died and he remarried, I became the stepchild. I had to provide for myself. When I heard this woman's story, I viewed her situation through my lens. However, that wasn't her story.

She feared being lonely. Her father, a successful medical doctor, amply supplied her material needs. But he was emotionally disconnected. She'd felt alone much of her life. She completely trusted God to meet her financial needs, but she doubted he would care for her emotional needs.

The apostle Paul said we see through a glass darkly (1 Cor. 13:12). Even if our church's doctrine was sound and our parents were loving, who, in this broken world, clearly sees God as he is? We interpret life through the distorted filters we built from childhood—one wound at a time.

However, there is hope. Even if, like Gideon, questioning comes easier than trust, we can bring our doubts to the Lord. Wrestling with God over our questions can strengthen our weak muscles.

God's Word heals us by exposing our flawed beliefs. When our perception doesn't align with his Word, we can choose to trust him over beliefs formed by pain.

Gideon's mustard seed of faith sprouted and grew with each exchange with the Lord. He named the altar he built "the LORD is peace" (Judg. 6:24). To sustain that peace, the next day, he needed a fresh connection with God. To experience vigorous faith, we, too, must daily abide in Christ.

Hebrews 11:34 (NLT) says Gideon "became strong in battle." His weakness turned to strength *as he fought* his fears and followed God's counterintuitive directions from preparation to attack. God wants to turn the wounds and weaknesses of our past into strength. This happens as we move forward by faith.

Scripture Reading..

"How much more do I need to say? It would take too long to recount the stories of the faith of Gideon, Barak, Samson, Jephthah, David, Samuel, and all the prophets. By faith these people overthrew kingdoms, ruled with justice, and received what God had promised them. They . . . escaped death by the edge of the sword. Their weakness was turned to strength. They became strong in battle and put whole armies to flight."[4] —Hebrews 11:32–34 (NLT)

JUDGES 7

Study and Reflection

1. Why did God trim Israel's army (Judg. 7:2)?

2. When Gideon told the men that those who trembled with fear could leave, 22,000 left. Only 10,000 stayed. What happened next (Judg. 7:3–8)?

3. If Gideon had been afraid of battling 135,000 (Judg. 8:10) with 32,000 soldiers, imagine how he felt with 300. Are you facing an impossible challenge? Apply God's reason for having Gideon pare down his troops to your battles. Why does God allow humanly impossible situations?

4. After reducing his troops from 32,000 to 300, Gideon may have wondered why he hadn't run home with the fearful! How did God further encourage him before battle (Judg. 7:9–14)?

5. A dream about a tumbling loaf of barley bread doesn't sound threatening. But the image terrified the Midianites and spurred Gideon to action. They understood the dream's meaning. God had given Gideon victory over Midian. Describe Gideon's immediate response and unusual battle plan (Judg. 7:15–25).

6. Why was Gideon's small army able to have victory over their massive enemy (Judg. 7:22)? Apply that to today.

7. God understood Gideon's weaknesses and supplied the help he needed to succeed in his assignment. Notice how our

High Priest deals with our weaknesses: "This High Priest of ours understands our weaknesses, for he faced all of the same testings we do, yet he did not sin. So let us come boldly to the throne of our gracious God. There we will receive his mercy, and we will find grace to help us when we need it most" (Heb. 4:15–16 NLT). Do you show mercy to others and yourself in times of weakness? How do God's dealings with Gideon challenge you in this area?

8. Record your final thoughts from today's lesson.

God Helps Us in Our Weaknesses

"If you started a church, what would you name it?" My friend's question startled me. But a name immediately came.

As I drove home, I reminded the Lord of our little strength and asked, "You can't be telling us to start a church, can you?"

The scripture, "I know that you have little strength," immediately came to mind. I couldn't wait to read the context.

I opened my Bible and read, "I know your deeds. See, I have placed before you an open door that no one can shut. I know that you have little strength, yet you have kept my word and have not denied my name" (Rev. 3:8). As I read further, the words continued to speak to me.

Over the next months, we couldn't avoid the stream of apparent indications that God wanted us to start a church. We resisted because we didn't see how this could be. My husband, Larry, had no desire to be a pastor. Neither of us had the energy to add something like this to our lives.

One day, after another apparent confirmation, I told Larry, "I feel we are being disobedient if we don't at least try."

He said, "If God wants me to start a church, I need someone to say to me, 'This area needs a church pastored by Larry Wilson.' Then I'll know it's God."

"If that is what you need, let's ask him." We did.

The next day we celebrated the Fourth of July with some friends in Southport, North Carolina. During lunch, an out-of-town friend who used to attend our Sunday school class years earlier stopped by our table. He pointed to Larry and said, "What Cary, North Carolina, needs is a church like the Walkers Class [our former Sunday school class] with Larry Wilson as the pastor."

Goose bumps ran up my arms as he walked away. We had told no one about our fleece.

You might think we were ready to open our doors after that. But we weren't sure what to do or how to begin. When I planned a meeting with friends to discuss it, Larry said he didn't feel that was the way. Yet both of us wanted others to join us and share the vision—and the load. One night before bed, I watched the end of a Christian TV program on interpreting dreams. I didn't think much of it. But that night, a vivid dream woke me.

I dreamed Larry and I sat in a jeep parked in a wooded area of our yard, not our driveway. Evergreen trees crowded us inside the jeep. The trees were lovely to look at, but they poked us and blocked our view. A friend stood beside the jeep and pulled out the larger evergreens. We felt relief with each removal. Finally, only one small tree remained in the back. This tree was especially sweet and didn't block our view. I wanted to keep it. However, I knew it had to go. Removing this tree hurt.

God had never spoken to me in a dream before, but I instantly understood the interpretation. Larry and I didn't own a jeep. It symbolized the off-road adventure God had called us to. Our journey would take us down unmarked paths.

The evergreen trees represented the mature believers Larry and I hoped would join us. We were hiding behind them. Instead of helping us on our journey, they would crowd us and block our vision. Like Gideon, we had to let our soldiers go.

Our friend who stood outside the jeep would support our venture, but she would not join us inside the jeep. The small tree that hurt when it was removed represented a close friend and ministry partner. She would be with us as we began, then leave.

The dream rang true for Larry also. We figured God wanted us to start, and he'd later supply a real pastor. But that wasn't God's path for us. Every time we thought of trying to build something, we felt an invisible but undeniable restraint. God had something different in mind. Like the empty jars that contained only torches, we had to empty ourselves of expectations and the traditions we associated with church. The Holy Spirit would fill us and light the way. Only later did we realize we were part of the Holy Spirit's movement to raise up home churches across our nation and the world.

Every aspect of the dream came true. We began without the leaders we'd hoped would join us. The small tree started with us but left. And her departure hurt. Everyone in our dream eventually joined us, including the one helping us outside the jeep. And the small tree returned.

Larry and I learned to trust the Lord in ways we never had before. This venture brought forth incredible spiritual growth in us as we walked this path with each other and the Lord. We learned to redefine church and success. God didn't want this to be like any church we'd ever been part of. He knew our strengths and weaknesses. He'd supply strength, people, and guidance as we went. Success was obeying God in the power of the Holy Spirit and leaving the results with him.

Isaiah 30:21 says, "Whether you turn to the right or to the left, your ears will hear a voice behind you, saying, 'This is the way; walk in it.'" I've found God often directs me as I go—after I surrender to him.

Today's Strength Builder

With whom do you need to empathize or show mercy in their weaknesses?

CLOSING PRAYER

Use this space to turn your insights and responses into prayers.

Day Five

God's Weapons: Foolish or Effective

A counseling professor relayed his experience with a client who suffered from agoraphobia that manifested itself in a fear of leaving home. The woman would schedule an appointment and set out to meet him on the appointed day. When her fear took over, she'd call and set another time to meet. Each week she made it a little further away from home. One day, she drove the whole way without fear. She'd conquered her phobia.

God sometimes uses unusual means of deliverance. He draws an enemy attack when we want him to drive it away. He made Moses confront Pharaoh, Israel face Pharaoh's chariots, and Gideon challenge Midian. And God does the same with us.

When a conversation unleashes negative thoughts, invites comparison, causes us to feel sorry for ourselves or taste the bitterness of an old grievance, or when an opponent intimidates us into silence when we should speak or provokes us to lash out when we should keep quiet, remember, God draws out our enemy to defeat him and deliver us.

As people overcome phobias by facing them, we become strong by walking with God through our struggles. Defeating, not retreating, brings genuine peace.

> For though we live in the world, we do not wage war
> as the world does. The weapons we fight with are not
> the weapons of the world. On the contrary, they have
> divine power to demolish strongholds. We demolish
> arguments and every pretension that sets itself up
> against the knowledge of God, and we take captive every
> thought to make it obedient to Christ. (2 Cor. 10:3–5)

The weapons God selected for Joshua and Gideon look foolish. Joshua marched, blew trumpets, and shouted in the battle of Jericho. Gideon used shouts, trumpets, and lanterns.

The Israelites used trumpets at war and on holy days. Trumpets summoned troops and signaled Israel's dependence on God.

> When you arrive in your own land and go to war against
> your enemies who attack you, sound the alarm with the
> trumpets. Then the LORD your God will remember you
> and rescue you from your enemies. Blow the trumpets
> in times of gladness, too, sounding them at your
> annual festivals and at the beginning of each month.
> And blow the trumpets over your burnt offerings and
> peace offerings. The trumpets will remind your God

of his covenant with you. I am the LORD your God.
(Num. 10:9–10 NLT)

God's weapons appear flimsy next to powerful enemies. What power do earthen jars filled with torches have against trained warriors wielding sharp blades? Yet God used these simple tools in the hands of three hundred untrained men to defeat 135,000 armed soldiers.

Paul wrote, "But we have this treasure in jars of clay to show that this all-surpassing power is from God and not from us" (2 Cor. 4:7). Paul also prayed "that the eyes of your heart may be enlightened in order that you may know . . . his incomparably great power for us who believe" (Eph. 1:18–19). Our power comes from knowing Jesus and allowing his Holy Spirit to fill and control every aspect of our lives. When we acknowledge our dependence on the Lord, sound the trumpet of truth, and shout God's praise, the Lord releases his strength in and through us. And we bring him glory.

Gideon Became a Warning When He Stopped Being an Example

When we fight in the strength God has provided, the Holy Spirit accomplishes much more than we can ask or imagine. But that doesn't stop Satan's schemes. After the great victory the Lord accomplished, Gideon built an ephod with gold from the booty they'd won. *The Quest Bible* notes, "Ephods were generally used by priests to discover God's will—a practice Gideon distorted into a form of pagan worship. Perhaps his earlier experiences of seeking specific direction from God later became an obsessive fault for Gideon. He went too far and apparently could not worship the Lord without a visible, material object."[5]

With the enemy subdued, Gideon's need for closeness with the Lord seemed to lessen. A quick, tangible answer trumped experiencing God. Despite this failing, the land enjoyed forty years of peace during his lifetime. Israel did not return to Baal worship until after Gideon's death.

In Hebrews, God chose to remember Gideon's faith, not his flaws. Gideon's story reminds us the enemy uses our own flesh as well as attacks from without. Until heaven, we must walk in the power of the Spirit if we are to enjoy victory over the flesh (Gal. 5:16).

Today we wrap up our look at Gideon.

Scripture Reading...
JUDGES 8

Study and Reflection

1. Armed with trumpets and pitchers to hide their lanterns, Gideon and his men became strong in battle and put whole armies to flight. With only 300 men, he pursued an army of 15,000 that had already lost 120,000 swordsmen (Judg. 8:4, 10–11). What do you learn from this?

2. Can you recall a time when God chose you for a daunting task? How did you change as you trusted or failed to trust God?

3. The angel of the Lord found Gideon in hiding and called him a mighty man of valor. Jonathan Cahn says, "God sees us not as we are, but as he called us to be. He gives you an identity not based on your past . . . but on your future, what you are

to become."[6] How can you apply the following biblical principles to your life when you feel like hiding?

a. "Let the weakling say, 'I am strong!'" (Joel 3:10).

b. "Each time he said, 'My grace is all you need. My power works best in weakness.' So now I am glad to boast about my weaknesses, so that the power of Christ can work through me" (2 Cor. 12:9 NLT).

c. "For God has not given us a spirit of fear and timidity, but of power, love, and self-discipline" (2 Tim. 1:7 NLT).

4. After defeating the enemy, Gideon returned to retaliate against those who hadn't aided him and his men when they were pursuing Israel's enemy and to avenge the death of his brothers. It isn't clear when his brothers were slain—perhaps in peaceful times since Gideon seems to have taken on the duty of the "avenger of blood" described in Deuteronomy 19:11–12. Or maybe, emboldened by his victory, he no longer felt the need to seek God's leading. From the booty, he erected a golden ephod. While Israel's priests wore the ephod like an apron to receive direction from Yahweh, pagan cultures erected ephods as idols. In the priestly garment, twelve precious stones representing the twelve tribes of Israel covered the ephod (Exod. 28:6–30; 30:2–21; Lev. 8:7–8). Two flat stones called the Urim and Thummim were attached to the front of the vest. In some supernatural way, God communicated his will to the high priests through them. Israel's

Aaronic priests were the only ones sanctioned to wear an ephod (Exod. 28:4). What effect did this ephod have on Israel (Judg. 8:27)?

5. What positive effect did Gideon have on Israel during his time as judge (Judg. 8:33–35)?

6. What warning and encouragement do you draw from Gideon's story?

7. Record your final thoughts from today's lesson.

How Do I Discern God's Will?

My husband talked to a young woman who seeks direction from tarot cards. These instant answers don't provide wisdom or God's will. Seeking God for direction may take time. But it clarifies our motives. Do we want an answer—or do we want God's will?

Gideon prepared a feast for the angel of the Lord and then, using a fleece, waited two additional nights to affirm God's calling. After experiencing God during wartime, Gideon substituted a golden ephod in peacetime for communication with God. Throwing dice may be easier than waiting on God, but only God knows what's best. We need him more than we need an answer. Challenges and decisions provide opportunities to experience the Lord as our helper and shepherd (Heb. 13:6; Ps. 23).

Gideon reminds me of a woman who asked me to pray she would know God's will on whether to marry her boyfriend. I learned she was already sleeping with him. She believed the blessing of a happy marriage was found in God's will. But she hoped to gain God's blessing outside his already revealed will (1 Thess. 4:3–5; Heb. 13:4).

Do you need help hearing from God? Consider the following biblical principles. Make them part of your lifestyle and use them when you face bigger decisions.

- Ask God to make you willing to do his will (John 7:17)
- Ask for wisdom believing he will lead you (James 1:5–8)
- Delight in the Lord and let him shape your desires (Ps. 37:4)
- Walk in the Spirit (Gal. 5:16)
- Study his Word (Ps. 119:105; Heb. 4:12)
- Wait for his peace (Phil. 4:7; Judg. 6:24)

The Lord promised to be with Gideon. Today, the Holy Spirit indwells all believers (Rom. 8:9). He helps, guides, comforts, and empowers us to live victorious lives. The Spirit uses God's timeless truths to instruct us through every stage of life. Willful disobedience stifles his work (1 Thess. 5:19).

When we earnestly seek God in faith, like Gideon, we experience his presence and discover a peace that surpasses comprehension (Phil. 4:6–9). However, jitters can accompany God's peace. We may feel empowered to move forward and still feel uneasy over the unknown.

Gideon's biggest enemy wasn't Midian. It was Gideon. The Lord patiently nurtured his struggling faith. He knows when we need reassurance and when we're making excuses. Don't be afraid to ask him for encouragement. Act on your faith. Faith grows strong through use.

Gideon's victory presented a different kind of snare. In his newfound confidence, Gideon apparently stopped seeking God directly. When the pressure's off, we, too, can be tempted to substitute religious rituals for a living relationship with God.

In his book *Through the Eyes of a Lion*, Levi Lusko wrote, "For every person who has been destroyed by suffering, there are probably ten who have been wrecked by success."[7] Let's learn from Gideon and remember we need Jesus just as much in peaceful times as in battles.

Today's Strength Builder

Seek God and his will—not just an answer.

CLOSING PRAYER

Use this space to turn your insights and responses into prayers.

Prayer Requests

Strength from Teamwork

Barak means "lightning" or "lightning flash."[1]

BARAK STUDIED DEBORAH. HE RESPECTED THIS WISE JUDGE and courageous prophet of God. But her summons rattled him. A showdown with Sisera sounded like a death wish. He was no match for this cunning general. Satan had deceived Eve. Could he have fooled Deborah?

He shook his head. No, every word Deborah had spoken from the Lord had proven true. "All right, I'll go. But," he looked her in the eye, "*only* if you go with me."

~

"Deborah rocks!" a gal from my Bible study exclaimed when we discussed this story. Yet, Hebrews 11 names Barak, not Deborah, as an example of faith. Was the author showing a chauvinistic bias? No, the same writer listed Rahab by name and not Joshua. In naming Barak, the writer showcased Deborah too. No one can read this story and miss Deborah's faith. But I, for one, would have overlooked Barak's faith if Hebrews 11 hadn't named him.

Hebrews 11 highlights Barak after Gideon even though this story chronologically comes first. The defeat of Jericho, two hundred years earlier, had become a faded memory. For twenty years, Israel languished under the oppression of a coalition of Canaanite rulers led by their intimidating general, Sisera. This week, we look at the unlikely team, Barak, Deborah, and Jael, that God used to stop these oppressors.

Day One
Partnering with God

"I do it." My toddler pushed my hand away. While it is healthy for children to show independence, believers never outgrow the need for God. How do you define spiritual maturity? Do you believe grown-up faith makes you less dependent on Christ? God created us to need him. As we never outgrow our need for air, healthy believers never lose their dependence on Jesus.

The first man, Adam, worked with God on his first day on earth, naming the animals. He rested with God on his second day. He got into trouble when he acted independently from God.

While on earth, Jesus said he did nothing by himself. He watched and joined his Father (John 5:19; 8:28). The apostle Paul wrote, "For to me, to live is Christ" (Phil. 1:21). He also said, "Christ lives in me. The life I now live in the body, I live by faith in the Son of God, who loved me and gave himself for me" (Gal. 2:20).

The more we mature in our faith, the more we rely on Jesus—and vice versa. And the better a nation honors God, the better it prospers (Prov. 14:34). Sadly, the reverse of this doesn't play out. The more ancient Israel prospered, the less she pursued God. The transference of faith from one generation to another is not automatic.

After God led Israel into the Promised Land, she drifted away from him. Later generations decided they didn't need him or his ways.

Each time Israel turned to foreign gods, God allowed foreign rulers to dominate her. The cycle of spurning God, suffering oppression, crying out to God, and receiving deliverance repeated itself over and over again.

It usually took *years* of suffering before Israel humbled herself and asked God for help. Every time she sincerely cried to the Lord, he provided a deliverer. Yet, a Spirit-anointed leader didn't eliminate the need to fight. Israel battled, and soldiers died.

Peace and prosperity followed under the new spiritual and political ruler. When that leader died, like a dog that returns to its own vomit, so Israel returned to idolatry (Prov. 26:11). And the cycle began again.

When we live independently from God, like Israel, we eventually crash. The Bible lights the straightest path to restoration. "Humble yourselves, therefore, under God's mighty hand, that he may lift you up in due time" (1 Pet. 5:6). Only then can we reclaim the ground we gave to our enemy.

Human nature and God have not changed. He is still jealous for his people. "Don't you realize that friendship with the world makes you an enemy of God? I say it again: If you want to be a friend of the world, you make yourself an enemy of God. . . . God is passionate that the spirit he has placed within us should be faithful to him" (James 4:4–5 NLT). May we learn from Israel's failings that we never outgrow our need for Jesus.

Scripture Reading..
DEUTERONOMY 9:4–6
JUDGES 2; 3:2–9, 12, 15; 4:1–3

Study and Reflection

1. God humbled Israel in the wilderness "so that in the end it might go well" with her (Deut. 8:16). If Israel thought her strength had achieved what God had accomplished for her, she would forsake him. When the time came to bring Israel into the Promised Land, God explained why he would give the land to Israel. Why did he drive the other nations out, and what do you take from this (Deut. 9:4–6)?

2. Before sending Israel into the land, he said, "The LORD your God will drive out those nations before you, little by little. You will not be allowed to eliminate them all at once, or the wild animals will multiply around you" (Deut. 7:22). What looked like slowness was divine protection. How do you apply this, especially when God's timetable doesn't match yours?

3. God gave Israel specific promises and warnings. Judges 2 provides background. According to Judges 2:1–3, 10–15, 19–23, why did God stop driving out the pagan nations from the Promised Land?

4. How would God use the nations that remained to test Israel (Judg. 2:22; 3:2, 4)?

5. How did Israel perform when tested (Judg. 3:5–6)?

6. What do you learn from the pattern found in Judges 3:7–9, 12, 15; 4:1–3?

7. Sin entices human nature like roadkill draws vultures. How do we protect ourselves from the deadening influence of a culture that celebrates sin?

8. Record your final thoughts from today's lesson.

Tested Faith Reveals Our Hearts

Before we built our house, we envisioned ambitious plans for our one-and-three-quarter acre lot. We soon realized we'd tackled too much landscape at once. While we tended the area around our house, the undergrowth in the woods grew back. We either had to become full-time gardeners or designate natural areas. Recognizing our limits helped us adjust our expectations and shed unnecessary responsibilities.

The Promised Land contained two potential snares: wild beasts and idolatry. If God drove out all the idol worshipers at once, wild animals would move in and attack Israel. If he let the Canaanites stay, the lure of idol worship would seduce Israel. The solution: drive out the idol worshipers, bit by bit, and warn Israel not to mix with those left.

The worship of Baal and his female cohort Asherah were the most prominent forms of worship in Canaan during this time.

The cult of Baal involved the offering of many animal sacrifices. Priests would officiate on behalf of the persons presenting sacrificial animals to the god. Some of the northern kingdom rulers even "made their sons pass through fire"—offering their own sons as sacrifices to Baal. "Holy prostitutes"—both male and female—were available to worshipers, encouraging the fertility of both land and people.[2]

The nation of Israel developed a lasting attraction to Baal, which eventually caused her downfall.

God sometimes allows our enemies to coexist with us. Coworkers with coarse tongues and crude lifestyles and neighbors who don't share our morals dwell beside us and our children. As Israel's neighbors tested them, these people try us.

My friend Amanda was in the seventh grade when a girl with a rough reputation spread the word she was coming after Amanda. Amanda told her father, and he replied, "Mandy, you're strong. You lift weights, and you've been swinging a tennis racket for years. You can handle that girl."

"I believed him," Amanda said. "So did the girl when I repeated my father's words to her. No one bothered me after that."

God wants his children to stand strong and fearless too. Conflict awakens us. We find out what we really believe. Randy Alcorn wrote, "The faith that can't be shaken is the faith that has been shaken."[3]

Living among people who mock our beliefs and morals compels us to discover what we really believe. Will we "keep the way of the Lord" (Judg. 2:22; 3:4) when doing so isolates or draws unfavorable attention? Or will we be swept up in the day's current (Judg. 2:3)? Submissively accepting the messages of books, music, movies, and TV shows that scoff biblical values dulls our discernment and bends our values and beliefs.

Defending our faith strengthens our faith muscles. We learn through practice to be calm and attentive when our children share the pressures they face. We provide a safe place for them to wrestle through their doubts and fears. Battles provide opportunities to search the Scriptures together and solidify what we believe.

> For someone who lives on milk is still an infant and doesn't know how to do what is right. Solid food is for those who are mature, who through training have the skill to recognize the difference between right and wrong. (Heb. 5:13–14 NLT)

Developing a love relationship with Jesus, not just a moral code of behavior, offers more protection than a list of dos and don'ts (2 Cor. 5:14). We and our children grow strong as we see ourselves as Christ's ambassadors called to speak the truth in love.

God created us to partner with him. If Israel had been faithful to God, at the right time he would have driven her enemies from the land. God would have used the nomads' temporary stay to strengthen his people. But, instead of smashing Baal's altars, God's people joined the idolatry. Their godless friends became their oppressors. They always do.

Darkness and light cannot mesh into one happy faith. We follow different gods. Partnering with false gods always leads us away from the one true God. But living among those who follow different gods clarifies what we truly believe.

Today's Strength Builder

Instead of focusing on your enemy, draw near to God.

CLOSING PRAYER

Use this space to turn your insights and responses into prayers.

Day Two

Pairing Faith with Action

Deborah means "honeybee."

> *"Some trust in chariots and some in horses,*
> *but we trust in the name of the LORD our God."*
> —Psalm 20:7

What distinguishes small faith from no faith? Action. "Faith by itself, if it is not accompanied by action, is dead" (James 2:17).

Jesus told his disciples after they'd failed to heal a boy suffering from seizures, "Truly I tell you, if you have faith as small as a mustard seed, you can say to this mountain, 'Move from here to there,' and it will move. Nothing will be impossible for you" (Matt. 17:20).

Jesus had given the disciples "authority to drive out impure spirits and to heal every disease and sickness" (Matt. 10:1). They only had to say, "Move from here to there," for it to move!

Our words have power, too (Prov. 18:21). Declaring Christ's promises ignites faith and infuses us with the courage to stand when we'd rather hide. Mustard seed–sized faith paired with action works wonders.

To be clear, Jesus wasn't saying we can speak our desires into existence. The New Age movement teaches that we're gods and our words create reality. The Bible teaches there is one God. Biblical faith doesn't rest in our ability to believe hard enough but in God's ability to keep his promises.

We partner with God by trusting him enough to follow his leading. He's chosen to link his work with our faith. In fact, Jesus didn't do many miracles in his hometown because of their unbelief (Matt. 13:58). God still partners with humans who walk by faith to build his kingdom and accomplish his will.

In response to God's Word, Moses held his staff over the Red Sea. Joshua marched around Jericho. Gideon sent away most of his troops. They obeyed, and God parted the sea, crumbled the walls, and routed the enemy.

Holding a staff can't split water unless God wills it. We don't study the Bible to learn strategies to replicate but to know God so we can recognize his voice and follow him in faith.

Dr. Neil T. Anderson wrote, "If God declares something to be true, you simply believe him and live according to what is true. If God didn't say it, no amount of faith in the world will make it so. Believing doesn't make God's Word true. His Word is true; therefore we believe it."[4]

In Hebrews chapter 11, God highlights a general who wouldn't battle a fierce enemy unless a particular wife and mother in Israel rode with him (Heb. 11:32). But with Deborah beside him, Barak charged into battle despite personal misgivings, and God applauded his faith. We can demonstrate God-pleasing faith even when doubts accompany our obedience.

Pastor and author Tony Evans said, "Faith is acting as if God is telling the truth."[5] Gideon and Barak obeyed God despite their uncertainty over themselves and the outcome. Faith gave this military leader the humility to ask Deborah for support. Instead of chiding him, Hebrews 11 commends him.

Scripture Reading..
JUDGES 4:1–10; 5:7

Study and Reflection

1. List Deborah's roles (Judg. 4:4–5; 5:1, 7).

2. What did the Lord promise through Deborah (Judg. 4:6–7)?

3. Why do you think Barak put a condition on obeying the Lord's command (Judg. 4:8)? What does this say about this military leader's respect for Deborah?

4. What outcome did Deborah predict (Judg. 4:9)?

5. Hebrews 11 lists Barak as a man of faith. Despite his reservations, he immediately obeyed God and fought Israel's fierce enemy. What do you learn about faith from Barak?

6. Deborah had spiritual and political insight and power, but she was no military leader. Barak lacked Deborah's vision and connection with God, but he could lead troops. What personal application do your draw from their example?

7. Record your final thoughts from today's lesson.

Strong Teamwork Makes Dreams Work

Have you ever looked at a capable leader and thought, *They don't need my help*? Deborah was a capable leader with a special connection with God. While most of Israel's judges distinguished themselves through military prowess, she gained Israel's respect by serving as a prophetess, a judge, and a worship leader.

As with Moses before her and the kings that would follow, Israel brought their disputes to Deborah to settle. They trusted her to speak God's wisdom. The Bible identifies her as Lappidoth's wife. Deborah called herself a mother of Israel. Although she lived in a patriarchal society, there seemed to be no conflict between her role as a wife and her serving as a spiritual and political leader.

Yet, even with all her strengths, Deborah needed help. She longed to free her people from oppression. But God had not called her to lead a military campaign. God answered the burden of her heart by identifying his chosen man to lead Israel's volunteers into battle.

Barak lacked Deborah's vision and spiritual discernment. But he could lead an army. With Deborah as his guide, he would lead the charge against Israel's mighty enemy.

Deborah and Barak illustrate the body of Christ at work. No one has all the spiritual gifts. We need each other. Wise leaders welcome those who are strong where they are weak. Under the direction of the Holy Spirit, we work together in harmony, and God does more than we can imagine (Eph. 3:20).

> A spiritual gift is given to each of us so we can help each other. . . . It is the one and only Spirit who distributes all these gifts. He alone decides which gift each person should have. (1 Cor. 12:7, 11 NLT)

God has gifted you for your role in his story. He makes no mistakes. When we compare ourselves with others, instead of exercising what we have, we and the body of Christ suffer.

If you're feeling frustrated, make sure you're not wearing a hat never meant for you. But also, make sure you don't shirk the one God has given you, even if it challenges you. As Deborah later sang, "When the princes in Israel take the lead, when the people willingly offer themselves—praise the LORD!" (Judg. 5:2).

Today's Strength Builder

What special gift or strength has God given you to benefit the body of Christ? If you don't know, ask three people who know you well for three words that best describe you.

CLOSING PRAYER

Use this space to turn your insights and responses into prayers.

Day Three
Experiencing a Big God

General Sisera smirked when he heard a woman was behind Israel's move to break free. He surveyed his troops and nine hundred iron chariots. It shouldn't take more than a day to squelch their rebellion.

But God had other plans. He unzipped the heavens, and the Kishon River flooded the valley, turning Sisera's heavy chariots into death traps. Barak's men swept down on them. Not a man from Sisera's troops survived.

Are you facing a problem too huge to handle? Do you hear your enemy's scoffs? Take heart from today's reading. Opportunities to experience a big God often come dressed as battles.

Scripture Reading..

JUDGES 4:11–23

"It would take too long to recount the stories of the faith of Gideon, Barak . . . and all the prophets. By faith these people . . . received what God had promised them. . . . Their weakness was turned to strength. They became strong in battle and put whole armies to flight." —Hebrews 11:32–34 (NLT)

Study and Reflection

1. Pain is our friend when it prompts life-giving change. After twenty years of oppression, Israel cried out to God (Judg. 4:3). I'm sure they grumbled during those twenty years, but like someone who complains about a toothache but refuses to see a dentist, they weren't ready to listen to God. Have you ever avoided God because you knew he'd require change? It's not wrong to seek relief; however, wanting relief should never replace seeking to be right with God. How do we substitute relief for closeness with the Lord?

2. God led Sisera to the Kishon River for Israel to defeat them (Judg. 4:7). But I bet Sisera thought he was in charge. When he heard Barak had gathered troops, "Sisera summoned from Harosheth Haggoyim to the Kishon River all his men and his nine hundred chariots fitted with iron" (Judg. 4:13). Barak led a group of volunteers who lacked shields and spears

and probably traveled by foot (Judg. 5:8–9). How did Barak demonstrate faith (Judg. 4:14)?

3. While Barak clearly demonstrated faith and courage (Judg. 4:12–23; 5:13–15), in the account found in Judges, Deborah and Jael appear to be the human heroes. Why do you think Hebrews 11:32 named Barak?

4. List the different roles God and Israel played as they partnered together in this battle (Judg. 4:10, 14–16, 23–24). What do you learn from this?

5. Record your final thoughts from today's lesson.

Exercising Small Faith

"Character is not something you were born with and can't change, like your fingerprint. In fact, because you weren't born with it, it is something that you must take responsibility for creating. . . . Character is built by how you respond to what happens in your life. Whether it's winning every game or losing every game."[6] —Jim Rohn

I was helping a client set healthy boundaries with a manipulative friend when her so-called friend turned her malice on me. She phoned several times a day and stayed silent when I answered. This was before caller ID. My voicemail confirmed her identity when it recorded her talking to her child.

The Lord tells us to bless our enemies and overcome evil with good. How do you bless someone you feel more like blasting? The next time my mute caller rang, I said, "God bless you, Jacklyn" (not her real name). This tiny step of obedience, ironically, erased my irritation. I felt empowered. The calls stopped soon after I started blessing my enemy.

Instead of pesky phone calls, perhaps annoying thoughts disrupt your peace. God allows us to be stirred so we'll call on him and receive healing at deeper levels. Satan may use the people in our lives to poke our sensitivities. The Lord allows those tender areas to be tapped to deliver us from our weaknesses.

> "No weapon forged against you will prevail, and you will refute every tongue that accuses you. This is the heritage of the servants of the LORD, and this is their vindication from me," declares the LORD. (Isa. 54:17)

Sisera appeared invincible. But when his men started to lose, he abandoned them (Judg. 4:17). Without his troops, he was as vulnerable as a kitten. When the enemy comes at you, face him in the strength of the Lord and watch your faith and character grow. Take the one step God shows you, and the next step will unfold. God draws out our enemies to glorify his name and deliver us.

Today's Strength Builder

What small step will you take today to face your challenge?

CLOSING PRAYER

Use this space to turn your insights and responses into prayers.

Day Four

Deborah and Jael: Joining the Right Team

Jael means "mountain goat."[7]

"Villagers in Israel would not fight; they held back until I,
Deborah, arose, until I arose, a mother in Israel."
—Judges 5:7

The meanings of Jael's and Deborah's names (mountain goat and honeybee, respectively) reminded one woman of the "milk and honey" of the Promised Land. These women brought sweetness to Israel, but Israel's enemy felt this honeybee's sting.

A good shepherd fights to protect the sheep (John 10:11–13) because passive acceptance of wrongdoing can be worse than an oppressive enemy. Just ask someone who grew up in an abusive home. Often children abused by one parent later harbor resentment against the passive parent who did nothing to stop the abuse.

While most judges distinguished themselves through military feats, Israel's only female judge gained respect through her wisdom and relationship with God. She was a mother, and like a good mother, she counseled and settled disputes under the Palm of Deborah and pointed her charge to the Lord.

Deborah served Israel as a judge or ruler and a prophetess. During this time, God directed Israel through his prophets. Deuteronomy told how to recognize God's Old Testament prophets:

> "But a prophet who presumes to speak in my name
> anything I have not commanded, or a prophet who
> speaks in the name of other gods, is to be put to death."
> You may say to yourselves, "How can we know when
> a message has not been spoken by the LORD?" If what
> a prophet proclaims in the name of the LORD does not

take place or come true, that is a message the LORD has
not spoken. That prophet has spoken presumptuously,
so do not be alarmed. (Deut. 18:20–22)

Deborah's record proved true.

It would have been easy to give in to hopelessness after living
twenty years under the heel of the Canaanites. But when Deborah
saw the oppression of her people and that no one resisted it, like
a mother hen, she stepped up to protect her charge (Judg. 5:7).
Under the Lord's guidance, she summoned Barak to lead the attack
against the Canaanites.

James wrote, "The earnest prayer of a righteous person has great
power and produces wonderful results" (James 5:16 NLT). Deborah's
guidance and inspiration moved Barak to summon troops from
Israel's clans. And God provided victory.

An Unexpected Teammate

Jael was a Kenite Gentile. "When the tribe of Judah left Jericho—
the city of palms—the Kenites, who were descendants of Moses's
father-in-law, traveled with them into the wilderness of Judah.
They settled among the people there, near the town of Arad in the
Negev" (Judg. 1:16 NLT).

While the Kenites were friends with Israel, Jael's husband,
Heber, chose to distance himself from his people and befriend
Israel's enemy (Judg. 4:11, 17). We don't know what motivated his
allegiance to the Canaanites. Perhaps survival. But God used this
alliance for his purposes and for Israel's good.

Sisera, who appeared fearless when surrounded by his troops,
abandoned his men when the battle turned against them. He
accepted Jael's invitation to hide in her tent. Her gracious welcome,
warm milk, and husband's alliance put him at ease. Battle weary,
he fell into a deep sleep (Judg. 5:25).

The Bible doesn't explain Jael's motives. To protect Sisera would support the friendship her husband's clan had with King Jabin. Yet God had promised to bless those who blessed Israel. Wouldn't it be better to stand with God's people? Her bold action not only ended this war but put her in God's book. Deborah and Barak praised her in their song of triumph (Judg. 5:24–27).

Deborah and Jael are bookends to Barak's story of faith. Deborah delivered the message that spurred Barak to attack the enemy. Jael ended the battle by killing the general. Let's look at what we can learn from these women.

Scripture Reading...
JUDGES 4:1–3, 6–9, 11, 16–24; 5:6–9, 24–27

Study and Reflection

1. What do you think it would have been like to live in Israel during this time of cruel oppression (Judg. 4:3)?

2. Have you, like Deborah, ever seen a problem but not had the means to fix it? I'm sure Deborah did not relish the risks, smells, sights, and sounds of battle. What two motivations moved Deborah to act (Judg. 4:6–9; 5:6–7)?

3. What woman fulfilled Deborah's prophetic words spoken in Judges 4:9?

4. Which of Deborah's traits stand out to you? How did she demonstrate faith?

5. List Jael's traits. Do you think Deborah's song indicates Jael acted in faith (Judg. 4:17–22; 5:24–27)?

6. What obstacles did Barak, Deborah, and Jael overcome, and how?

7. How does this chapter apply to you and to our culture? Record your final thoughts from today's lesson.

An Unlikely Ally

Despite her husband's alliance with the Canaanite rulers, Jael sided with Israel against Sisera. Was her husband's alliance only perfunctory? Were Jael's actions motivated by a sense of survival? What we do know is both Deborah and Barak praised her actions. Let's imagine the scene together.

Jael knew the Canaanites' cruelty. For her husband's sake—and their mutual survival—she played the welcoming hostess when the Canaanites came around. But she didn't trust them—or like them.

What was happening in the battle? Dare she hope the downpour had slowed Sisera's chariots?

A lone man stumbled toward her tent. Sisera! She stepped to greet him. "Come into my tent, sir. Don't be afraid."

"Water," he said.

She grabbed a skin of milk and a blanket. "Rest. I'll stand guard."

Soon, heavy breathing let her know he was asleep. Now what? If she waited for the Israelite soldiers, he might escape. Her eyes searched the tent for inspiration and landed on her hammer and tent pegs. A gruesome plan formed in her mind. She shuddered.

With tools in hand, Jael crept toward sleeping Sisera. She hesitated only long enough to recall his haughtiness and recent cruelty.

What mundane task have you done so often that you no longer think about how to do it? I've fed my dogs so many times that some days I check their bowls to be sure I fed them. Who'd have thought years of securing tent pegs would prepare a woman to defeat a war general? The ancients considered it an honor to kill your enemy's leader. This honor went to Jael, not Barak, as Deborah had predicted. The victory gave Israel forty years of peace, twice as many years of peace as oppression.

When you're faithful in your everyday roles, you please God—whether he ever calls you to heroic feats or not. However, those mundane tasks may prepare you for such a time as what these heroines experienced.

If life had been easy, we wouldn't be reading these women's stories. Dark backdrops showcase diamonds and faith. As Deborah sang, "May all who love you be like the sun when it rises in its strength" (Judg. 5:31).

Today's Strength Builder

Is there an area where you need to switch sides to join the Lord and his people?

CLOSING PRAYER

Use this space to turn your insights and responses into prayers.

Day Five

God Uses the Weak

"God wants weak vessels,
and that is the only kind he will use."[8]
—J. Vernon McGee

Have you noticed a theme running through our study? God chooses the weak. Clever and strong characters like Wonder Woman, played by Gal Gadot, and The Equalizer, played by Denzel Washington, fit many people's ideas of real heroes. But God often chooses leaders that are neither naturally clever nor strong.

> Brothers and sisters, think of what you were when you were called. Not many of you were wise by human standards; not many were influential; not many were of noble birth. But God chose the foolish things of the world to shame the wise; God chose the weak things of the world to shame the strong. God chose the lowly things of this world and the despised things—and the things that are not—to nullify the things that are, so that no one may boast before him. (1 Cor. 1:26–29)

Faith isn't impulsively rushing into trouble. Proverbs warns against that. Neither is it feeling confident. Faith is revering God enough to do what he says.

Jesus told a parable of two brothers to illustrate this (Matt. 21:28–32). A father asked his two sons to go and work in the vineyard. The first son refused, but later he changed his mind and went. The second son said, "Sure," but never went.

Jesus asked which son did his father's will. "The first," they correctly answered.

Obedience—not Bible knowledge, church attendance, the condition of our nerves, or the eagerness of our response—reveals God-pleasing faith. Even if you feel as fragile as a bubble, it doesn't matter. It takes more courage to act when we feel weak. Tenuous feelings may indicate you're on the right path!

Moses needed Aaron. Gideon needed a sign—or three. Barak needed Deborah. But each one obeyed God and experienced transformation as they went.

We may not be called to battle a fierce army, but we face self-defeating thoughts. We fear a relationship won't improve, a loved-one won't come to the Lord, or we'll never escape bad debt or poor health. Some days, hope sags like week-old balloons. But if we fill our minds with biblical truth, God will revive us. What he says is more reliable than the stories our circumstances tell us.

Scripture Reading...
Judges 4:6–7, 23–24; 5:1–31

Study and Reflection

1. Those who've lived in areas with no rule of law understand what Israel suffered. Name some of Israel's problems before Deborah arose (Judg. 5:2, 7–8).

2. Describe Barak's army (Judg. 5:8b–9, 13–18). Who didn't fight?

3. How does Deborah's song describe what turned the battle (Judg. 5:4–5, 20–21)?

4. "By faith these people . . . received what God had promised them" (Heb. 11:33 NLT). What did Barak receive that God had promised (Judg. 4:6–7, 23–24)?

5. Is there an area where you feel like Barak before the battle? Is there a Deborah in your life you can invite to help you step out in faith? For whom can you be a Deborah?

6. Record your final thoughts from today's lesson and what you learned about God in this story.

The Power of Teamwork

"March on, my soul; be strong!" —Judges 5:21

The many military examples in Hebrews 11 remind us life is a battle-ground, not a playground. Jesus has sent us into Satan's domain with the command and authority to make disciples (Matt. 28:18–20). He promised the gates of hell would not prevail against us (Matt. 16:18).

The story of Barak and Deborah depicts how the church is meant to work. We need each other—male and female—in this battle to rescue the perishing and set the captive free.

If Barak had lost this battle, Israel's mothers would have been lamenting the lives of their young soldiers and the loss of their daughters. The scene imagining Sisera's mother describes what her son and his men would have done if they had won. "Are they not finding and dividing the spoils: a woman or two for each man, colorful garments as plunder for Sisera" (Judg. 5:30).

Spiritual battles carry high stakes too. Our enemy still seeks to steal, kill, and destroy. But, as Kelly's following experience shows, believers working together save lives.

Kelly's Story

Growing up in an abusive home left Kelly feeling empty. She tried to fill the void with relationships. When she became pregnant, her parents, grandparents, and boyfriend pressured her to abort her baby. Only her brother said not to.

Kelly checked into the hospital as Jane Doe. She didn't want to embarrass her physician dad. Sister Joan, a thoughtful nun, listened to Kelly and provided a list of contacts if Kelly needed help with her difficult decision.

Kelly scheduled an abortion and wrote in her journal: "Lord, please intervene if this is wrong. . . . Please give me a sign. . . . My time is running out."

At the Pregnancy Resource Center, Kelly met Dawn from Sister Joan's list. She offered options and resources to help if Kelly decided to keep her baby or place her for adoption.

Her brother's friend wanted to help. He introduced her to Kathy—their state's top director of pro-life marches. "Kathy believed I could do this—and would help me. I canceled the abortion and wrote: 'Thank you, Lord, for coming through for me.'"

Naysayers

Kelly's friends said she was foolish to consider raising a child alone. Old fears resurfaced and churned Kelly's insides. She wanted to die. But Kathy kept her word, even spoon-feeding Kelly water. An OB/GYN offered to pay for Kelly's medical care and vitamins. Under his guidance, Kathy nursed Kelly back to health and connected her with Sue.

Sue worked in a ministry that helped women suffering from post-abortion trauma. "We watched an ultrasound video of a baby sucking its thumb in the womb, and I learned Sue's abortion had left her grieving and sterile. Kathy also introduced me to Karol, a pregnancy center counselor—also on Sister Joan's list."

I Found Hope

Despite all this, Kelly still struggled with uncertainty. On August 13, 1990, over the phone with Sue, Kelly invited Jesus into her heart. "After I hung up, I felt lighter. I felt joy. God loved me and would care for us. I had new strength, a close friend, and a heavenly Father to look out for me and my baby. I'd found the missing piece."

Sue and three other women rallied to support, mentor, and disciple Kelly. "God had given me a new family—the family of God."

A Baby Girl

"Sue, Karol, and my mom stood beside me when I delivered my 9 lb. 10 ounce, 21-inch-long beautiful daughter—Lauren Rose! I gave Kathy a dozen red roses to thank her, not realizing the pro-life symbol is a red rose.

"On Lauren's birthday, 2/25/91, my Bible calendar quoted Psalm 127:3, 'Children are a heritage from the Lord, offspring a reward from him'—one more sign of God's love. I can say Jesus is a father to the fatherless and husband to the husbandless. He used my daughter's birth to bring me spiritual life and a new forever family."

⌒

Look how many people played essential roles in Kelly's story. What if her brother hadn't encouraged her to resist their parents' pressure? What if Sister Joan had been too busy to listen to Kelly? What if her brother's friend hadn't reached out? What if Kathy had shrunk back from tending someone so ill? What if Sue hadn't allowed God to turn her past regret into a mission?

Each one performed an indispensable role in Kelly's and Lauren Rose's lives. You matter in God's story too. Never minimize the power of a word or action. We need you!

Today's Strength Builder

Who has played an essential role in your story? Have you thanked him or her?

CLOSING PRAYER

Use this space to turn your insights and responses into prayers.

Prayer Requests

Strength from Dedication

JEPHTHAH'S CHEST TIGHTENED. THE APPROACH OF HIS HALF brothers ganged together couldn't be good. The youngest stared at an invisible spot on the ground, avoiding eye contact.

"You need to leave. Now." The ringleader punched the air with his finger. "No son of a prostitute will share in our father's inheritance. You're an embarrassment to the family. A mistake that should never have been born."

Have people you counted on ever turned against you? Sometimes families (blood and spiritual) abandon their own. The psalmist understood this. "Though my father and mother forsake me, the LORD will receive me" (Ps. 27:10).

This week we look at Jephthah and Samuel, two leaders from Hebrews 11 who were dedicated to God but overlooked by the people who should have valued them. "God chose things the world considers foolish in order to shame those who think they are wise. And he chose things that are powerless to shame those who are powerful" (1 Cor. 1:27 NLT).

Day One
This Song's for You

As children, we'd recite this little ditty: "Pete and Repeat were in a boat. Pete fell out. Who was left?"

"Repeat," the other rang out.

The first person would repeat the verse. This could go on and on ad nauseam.

Are you tired of reading about Israel's constant rebellion? Me too. Judges could be summed up with this:

- Israel shunned God and pursued foreign gods.
- God let foreign people crush Israel.
- Israel cried for help.
- God sent a deliverer.
- Israel enjoyed peace.
- Repeat!

Thus, the account of Jephthah begins, "Again the Israelites did evil . . . . [The Lord] sold them into the hands of [their enemies]" (Judg. 10:6–7). Israel's fickleness continues to test God's faithfulness.

Why does God record this repetitive tale of failure? Do we need to hear it again?

Romans 15:4 says, "For everything that was written in the past was written to teach us, so that through the endurance taught in the Scriptures and the encouragement they provide we might have hope."

God records Israel's repeated flops and his countless rescues to instruct us and provide hope when we fail. By studying Israel, we learn the serious consequences of forsaking God and where to turn when we fall.

When Israel abandoned God for the false gods of other nations, God let those nations rule over Israel. Not because he'd given up on her, but to bring Israel to her senses. Because of his promise to Abraham, Isaac, and Jacob, God will never forsake Israel.

God remains faithful to his church too (2 Tim. 2:13). Yet, like in the days of Judges, not all who claim to worship God belong to him (Matt. 7:21). Private actions reveal true loyalties (Luke 6:46). Let's review Scripture's warning, so we won't repeat Israel's folly:

> You adulterers! Don't you realize that friendship with the world makes you an enemy of God? I say it again: If you want to be a friend of the world, you make yourself an enemy of God. Do you think the Scriptures have no meaning? They say that God is passionate that the spirit he has placed within us should be faithful to him. (James 4:4–5 NLT)

Scripture Reading...
JUDGES 10:6–18

Study and Reflection

1. From Judges 10:6–10, why was Israel in danger again? What two sins did Israel confess (Judg. 10:10)?

2. Israel forsook God to serve the Baals. Today, we're encouraged to gratify our impulses and feelings. According to Romans 6:16, why is indiscriminately obeying our urges dangerous? "Don't you realize that you become the slave of whatever you choose to obey? You can be a slave to sin,

which leads to death, or you can choose to obey God, which leads to righteous living" (NLT).

3. Christ broke sin's ruthless power over us when he died for our sins and rose from the grave. Using Romans 6:16 in the previous question and the following verses, how do we live free from sin's grasp?

    a. "Thank God! Once you were slaves of sin, but now you wholeheartedly obey this teaching we have given you. Now you are free from your slavery to sin, and you have become slaves to righteous living" (Rom. 6:17–18 NLT).

    b. "So I say, walk by the Spirit, and you will not gratify the desires of the flesh" (Gal. 5:16).

4. Israel ran out of "Get out of jail free" passes. Through an unnamed prophet, God named seven groups he'd delivered Israel from. The number seven represents completeness. How did God respond to Israel's cry for help (Judg. 10:11–14)?

5. God knew rescuing Israel before she repented would not help her in the long run. What did Israel do differently in Judges 10:15–16 that prompted God's help?

6. In the following verse, circle the conditions (our part) and underline God's promises when we do our part. "If my

people, who are called by my name, will humble themselves and pray and seek my face and turn from their wicked ways, then I will hear from heaven, and I will forgive their sin and will heal their land" (2 Chron. 7:14).

7. What lesson do you draw from comparing Judges 10:16 with the following? "Just as you used to offer yourselves as slaves to impurity and to ever-increasing wickedness, so now offer yourselves as slaves to righteousness leading to holiness. . . . But now that you have been set free from sin and have become slaves of God, the benefit you reap leads to holiness, and the result is eternal life. For the wages of sin is death, but the gift of God is eternal life in Christ Jesus our Lord" (Rom. 6:19, 22–23).

8. Record your final thoughts from today's lesson.

What Does It Look Like to Return to God?

The gathering of millions worldwide to pray during the 2020 pandemic and riots in America heartened me. However, following those days of prayer and fasting, unrighteousness ruled with new fury. Distortions from both political sides filled the airways. "Lord, you've promised to lift us up when we humble ourselves before you," I said. "What's going on?"

During this time, a horrible scandal involving a respected Christian leader broke. He'd silenced those who knew about his actions with threats that exposing him would ruin God's work. It's bad enough when any leader breaks trust, but to use God's name to cover sin is a thousand times worse. Such hypocrisy rocks believers and embitters unbelievers.

Isaiah describes how Israel called for days of fasting but showed no subsequent repentance:

> For day after day they seek me out; they seem eager to know my ways, as if they were a nation that does what is right and has not forsaken the commands of its God. They ask me for just decisions and seem eager for God to come near them. . . .
>
> Yet on the day of your fasting, you do as you please and exploit all your workers. Your fasting ends in quarreling and strife, and in striking each other with wicked fists. (Isa. 58:2–4)

The chapter goes on to describe how the Lord wants his people to experience the joy that is found only in honoring him (Isa. 58:11, 13–14).

Pagan gods drew the Hebrews away from God into destructive lifestyles and allegiances (Num. 25:1–3). Israel looked to Baal instead of Yahweh to bless their crops and herds. Asherah, Baal's female cohort, sanctioned immoral indulgence in sensual pleasure with ritual sex. Baal and Molech demanded the sacrifice of live human babies (Jer. 19:5).

Do you see the parallels to our culture? We look to our jobs instead of God to feed and clothe us (Matt. 6:24–34). The priests and priestesses of our culture (celebrities, sports figures, and educators) promote and celebrate sexual immorality through entertainment and pseudo-health education programs. This sexual explosion has led to the killing of millions of babies through abortion and the shattering of many souls. Are we any different from Israel?

God's judgment sometimes consists in giving people what they want (Rom. 1:18–32). To rescue Israel from the consequences of her sin before she turned from it wouldn't save her. Sin enslaves and destroys. Israel needed to do more than connect her pain with her choices. She needed to return to God.

We're called to pray for the world and our leaders, but we're also called to turn from our sin and put God first. Lesser gods vie for our loyalty. What do we sacrifice for titles and higher wages? Do we let video games and social media replace engagement with real people? Do we bend our values for a moment of relief or pleasure? Our spiritual enemy never sleeps.

A compromise here leads to callousness there. The best way to protect our nation, families, and ourselves is to wholeheartedly dedicate ourselves to the Lord. His Spirit supplies the power and the desire to walk in a manner worthy of our calling.

Are you ready to stop the "repeat" jingle and sing a new song? Ask God for a willing heart to follow him. Dedicate yourself to obeying him in every detail of your life (Phil. 2:12–13). The desire and strength to obey will grow with each step.

Today's Strength Builder

God stepped in when Israel turned from seeking relief to seeking him. Do any of the following areas need your attention? Humble yourself, pray, seek the Lord's face, and turn from your wicked ways.

CLOSING PRAYER

Use this space to turn your insights and responses into prayers.

Day Two
Dedicated to Truth

Jephthah means "he opens."[1]

I was around seven when I headed out of town to spend a weekend with an older cousin I admired. The weekend I'd anticipated quickly turned sour. My aunt and uncle were going through a messy divorce. Their daughter's nightmare spewed out on me. She spit in my spaghetti, bent my fingers back, and falsely accused me. Our adult supervisor, sympathizing with my cousin's hurt, overlooked her meanness and showed her special favor. This intensified her persecution.

My miserable weekend provided a small peek into what Jephthah's formative years must have been like. Jephthah was the son of Gilead and a prostitute who was probably a pagan. Moses's law banned illegitimate children from the assembly of God (Deut. 23:2). If that wasn't humiliating enough,

> Gilead's wife also bore him sons, and when they were
> grown up, they drove Jephthah away. "You are not going
> to get any inheritance in our family," they said, "because
> you are the son of another woman." So Jephthah fled
> from his brothers and settled in the land of Tob, where
> a gang of scoundrels gathered around him and followed
> him. (Judg. 11:2–3)

After his family rejected him, Jephthah became the leader of a group of scoundrels. God used Jephthah's hard times to train him for greater purposes. When the Ammonites threatened the area of Gilead, Jephthah's half brothers turned to him for help.

The angel of the Lord commissioned Gideon directly. The Lord spoke to Barak through the prophetess Deborah, but Jephthah's call came from the brothers who had rejected him.

Jephthah could have refused the men who had driven him away. On the other hand, a man starved for acceptance might have jumped to prove himself. But Jephthah did neither. He shrewdly made sure that if he led them in war, they would follow him in peace.

While Gideon received repeated assurances of victory, a sense of duty seemed to compel Jephthah. God chose this outcast, instead of one of his pedigreed brothers, to lead his people. Jephthah showed many good qualities, but he also made a foolish vow. We'll look at that tomorrow.

Scripture Reading..

"It would take too long to recount the stories of the faith of...Jephthah."
—Hebrews 11:32 NLT

JUDGES 11:1–33

"Do not conform to the pattern of this world, but be transformed by the renewing of your mind. Then you will be able to test and approve what God's will is—his good, pleasing and perfect will." —Romans 12:2

"The weapons we fight with are not the weapons of the world. On the contrary, they have divine power to demolish strongholds. We demolish arguments and every pretension that sets itself up against the knowledge of God, and we take captive every thought to make it obedient to Christ." —2 Corinthians 10:4-5

Study and Reflection

1. What do you learn about Jephthah in Judges 11:1–3?

2. Why did his brothers approach him, and how did he respond (Judg.11:4–11)?

3. How did the Ammonite king try to justify his attack on Israel (Judg. 11:12–13)?

4. What did Jephthah try first to avoid war (Judg. 11:14–27)?

5. Knowing Israel's history strengthened Jephthah's resolve to resist the Ammonites. Relate this story to your spiritual battles. Have you ever allowed an untrue narrative to manipulate you into giving up something you valued? How does knowing the truth about our identity and inheritance in Christ protect us (Judg. 11:23–24)?

6. A woman who'd suffered from relentless depression for six years told me her story of tragic loss. She'd prayed for years and found no relief from her grief and depression. When she learned to wage war in her mind and train her thoughts to obey Christ (2 Cor. 10:3–5), her countenance lifted. The Lord granted Jephthah a great victory (Judg. 11:28–33). But before receiving victory, like this woman, Jephthah did more than pray for victory. He fought for it (Judg. 11:32). From Romans 12:2 and 2 Corinthians 10:4–5, how do we fight a bad habit, attitude, or other internal battle?

7. Record your final thoughts from today's lesson.

Dedicated to Act

Rejection stings. But rejection for selfish gain from family or a trusted inner circle wounds at a whole new level. Jephthah's brothers didn't believe Jephthah deserved so much as a goat skin flask from their father's estate. Did greed drive them, or were they jealous of their warrior half brother? Perhaps Jephthah's illegitimacy embarrassed them. Whatever their motivation, their hostility sent Jephthah flying.

A college student once told me she felt the Lord had temporarily stripped away her friends to teach her to enjoy his presence. Perhaps being ostracized gave Jephthah a special awareness of God and a desire to please him. He seemed to practice a God-consciousness that others lacked (Judg. 11:11, 30).

God chose this outcast to lead his people and acknowledged Jephthah in Hebrews 11. Unlike Gideon, Jephthah was a mighty warrior when his brothers summoned him to lead them against the Ammonites. Despite his fighting experience, or perhaps because of it, he wisely tried to avert war with a rational appeal to the king of Ammon.

The king revised history to justify his aggression. Jephthah corrected the king's lies, but the king wanted the land Israel had possessed for three hundred years and refused to back down (Judg. 11:13–28).

If Jephthah had believed the king's shaming lies about his claim to the land, he might have surrendered the land to the Ammonites without a fight. If he had believed his brothers' early assessment of him, he would have lacked the courage to lead them. Our enemy also lies to steal our calling. Like Jephthah, we must refute arguments against God and his promises (Isa. 54:17). We must know the truth before we can declare, "Whatever the Lord our God has given us, we will possess."

Winning the battle began with knowing and speaking the truth. Jephthah followed his words with action. He showed up to the battle, and the Lord gave him victory. We must know the truth, and our actions must align with the truth.

One day, a friend asked the Lord how he saw her. "Overcomer" came to mind. Because she works in a political setting with people who hold strong differences in opinions and values, this word gave her confidence to be true to herself and her faith. The truth of how God saw her empowered her to stand strong in the presence of opposition. She didn't have to argue. She only had to speak and live as if what God says is true and let him bring the victory.

Passivity doesn't produce victory. We pray, we seek God's face—not just a break from our pain—and we fight in the strength of the Lord by taking every thought captive and living according to the truth. God wants us to fully possess all he's given us.

Today's Strength Builder

Whose assessment of your situation do you believe?

CLOSING PRAYER

Use this space to turn your insights and responses into prayers.

Day Three

Be Careful What You Promise

Returning from a resounding victory, Jephthah should have felt only joy. Instead, tension knotted his stomach as he remembered his vow. Who or what would exit his house first?

He gasped when his only child danced out the door, jingling her tambourines. She'd been watching for him, ready to celebrate her beloved father's safe return.

> "Oh no, my daughter! You have brought me down and I am devastated. I have made a vow to the LORD that I cannot break."
>
> "My father," she replied, "you have given your word to the LORD. Do to me just as you promised, now that the LORD has avenged you of your enemies, the Ammonites. But grant me this one request," she said. "Give me two months to roam the hills and weep with my friends, because I will never marry." (Judg. 11:35–37)

Jephthah had promised to sacrifice to the Lord whatever came out of his house if the Lord granted him victory. Some commentators believe that because of his mixed background of faith and paganism, Jephthah sacrificed his daughter as a burnt offering. The text can certainly be read that way. However, there is another possible interpretation. Let's consider both.

The book of Judges records many distressing stories of how low people who know God but set aside his ways can sink. A person's understanding of God affects how they interpret Scripture and life. Unfortunately, people of faith can hold distorted views of God, especially when they let traditions and superstitions supplant biblical truth. Some superstitions appear harmless, like knocking on wood to ward off misfortune. Others lead to death.

Foreign gods like Chemosh demanded human sacrifices. If Jephthah sacrificed his daughter as a burnt offering, he'd certainly confused Yahweh with the foreign gods around him. Sadly, if this is the case, he wasn't the last. Misplaced zeal drove Paul to persecute and kill Christians before he met Jesus on the road to Damascus. Religious leaders instigated the crucifixion of God's own Son.

Even today, some churches teach religious traditions as if they are biblical absolutes. People confuse legalistic commitment to their tradition with dedication to God. Religious legalists still persecute those who follow Christ instead of their rigid rules (Gal. 4:29).

The corruption among the clergy in the sixteenth century distressed William Tyndale. He believed if people could read the Bible themselves, they would no longer tolerate exploitation by the church. He set his energy to translating the Greek Bible into English.[2]

The church leaders accused Tyndale of heresy. Tyndale pressed through the resistance, published the English Bible in 1526, and began translating the Hebrew Old Testament. Church officials burned thousands of copies of the English Bible, and with the support of King Henry VII, they threw Tyndale into prison. They eventually burned him alive for heresy. He was only forty-two.[3]

Worshiping in Truth

Jesus said we are to worship in spirit and in truth (John 4:24). Such worship requires a clear understanding of God. Jesus also said he came to show us the Father. He replaced the harsh authoritarian God the Pharisees taught by revealing a compassionate Father who loves and restores prodigals. The prophet Micah showed how Israel's God differed from foreign gods:

What can we bring to the LORD? Should we bring him
burnt offerings? . . .

> Should we sacrifice our firstborn children to pay for
> our sins?

> No, O people, the LORD has told you what is good,
> and this is what he requires of you: to do what is right,
> to love mercy, and to walk humbly with your God.
> (Micah 6:6–8 NLT)

When Jephthah's daughter danced out to greet him, love for his
daughter should have given him pause. How would sacrificing his
daughter honor Israel's God? When he realized how his reckless
vow would impact her, he could have confessed his foolishness and
asked for forgiveness. Making his daughter pay for his foolishness
was wrong.

Jephthah's story provides a sober warning. Innocents do pay
for others' misguided mistakes, even if not directly. One's ignorance
and foolishness rarely impact just them. A parent's wrong view of
God can harm their children. On the other hand, humility and a
right relationship with the Lord will bless our loved ones (Ps. 112:2).
May this story prod us to do right, love mercy, and walk humbly
with our God.

Another Possibility

The Ryrie Study Bible notes that the latter part of Judges 11:31—"whatever comes out of the door of my house to meet me . . . will be the
LORD's, and I will sacrifice it as a burnt offering"—may be translated: "shall surely be the Lord's (if a human being comes first), or
I will offer it up for a burnt offering (if an animal appears first)."[4]
So while some Bible scholars hold that Jephthah offered his daughter as a burnt offering according to Canaanite practices, others

believe he dedicated his daughter into a life of service and celibacy and she was not slain.

Jephthah's message to the king of the Ammonites showed an impressive knowledge of Israel's history under Moses. With that knowledge, it seems he would have known the Law of Moses strictly forbade human sacrifice (Deut. 12:31; 18:10, 12). The law made provision for people and animals dedicated to the Lord to be redeemed or set apart for a lifetime of service (Lev. 27). While God instructed Joshua to destroy every living thing in Jericho for the Lord (Josh. 6:21), such dedications seem to have been instigated by God, not by individuals, and made in a national context involving defeated enemies (1 Sam. 15:3–21).[5]

Years after Jephthah, Hannah dedicated her son Samuel to the Lord. She brought the boy to Eli, Israel's high priest (1 Sam. 1:24–28). Samuel served the Lord his whole life.

Jephthah's daughter asked for time to mourn "because she would never marry." If she was about to be killed, I think she would have mourned her pending death. Jephthah's daughter, who obviously wanted marriage and children, would spend her life assisting "the priests in non-ceremonial duties connected with the sanctuary."[6] She showed amazing regard for her father and God's sovereignty in the jolting end to her plans.

Jephthah's half brothers had previously run him off. Who knows whether his military victory created any familial closeness? He was not part of his mother's clan. Dedicating his daughter meant Jephthah would have no grandchildren or son-in-law. "It represented the termination of the clan of Jephthah himself, since she was his only child."[7]

Hebrews 11 remembers Jephthah as one "who through faith conquered kingdoms, administered justice" (v. 33). Let's hope his faith and administration of justice extended to his daughter.

Scripture Reading...
JUDGES 11:30–31, 34–40
MICAH 6:6–8
1 CORINTHIANS 7:32–35

Study and Reflection

1. Throughout history, people have used religion to justify god-less actions. What do you learn about God from Micah 6:6–8?

2. Supposing Jephthah's dedication of his daughter meant she would live the rest of her life single in service to God (Judg. 11:37–39), list the benefits singleness provides (1 Cor. 7:32–35).

3. Some of God's people were made eunuchs to serve pagan kings (2 Kings 20:18). Infertility, death, and illness also snatched dreams of having children. In the New Testament, some believers lived as slaves to unbelieving masters. Even when we don't have control over our circumstances, we still have options. God rewards those who live by his principles. One reward is joy. What guiding principle do you draw from the following? "Whatever you do, work at it with all your heart, as working for the Lord, not for human masters, since you know that you will receive an inheritance from the Lord as a reward. It is the Lord Christ you are serving" (Col. 3:23–24).

4. What warning do you take from the following? "Don't trap yourself by making a rash promise to God and only later counting the cost" (Prov. 20:25 NLT).

5. What provision did the Mosaic law provide for rash vows? "The LORD spoke to Moses, 'Tell the Israelites: If any of you makes a special vow to give a person to the LORD, you may give money instead of the person'" (Lev. 27:1–2 GW).

6. Jesus addressed the misuse of vows. What do you learn from him? "Again, you have heard that it was said to the people long ago, 'Do not break your oath, but fulfill to the Lord the vows you have made.' But I tell you, do not swear an oath at all" (Matt. 5:33–34).

7. Record your final thoughts from today's lesson.

Consider before You Vow—Warnings and Instructions

"Would you like to go to the pool?" my young son asked.

"Sounds fun," I said, meaning that sounded nice—someday. I didn't see this as a promise for that day. I learned that my son did.

Jephthah made a reckless oath. Yet, he understood something our culture ignores. God takes vows seriously. God keeps his promises, and he wants his people to keep theirs.

One commentator wrote, "In Old Testament times vows were regarded as extremely serious acts (cf. Deut. 23:21–23), and the precautions listed here were meant to dissuade overenthusiastic and unrealistic vows. . . . Only those vows that conformed to the covenantal ethos would be acceptable to God."[8]

Moses's law provided a way out of impetuous oaths. Jephthah may not have understood that provision. He kept his oath at great personal cost in an age when Israel thought nothing of breaking their vow of faithfulness to God. Jephthah is commended for his faith—not for his oath. Because God is pleased with someone's faith doesn't mean he approves of everything they do.

Sometimes, people say "I swear" in casual conversations. This may seem innocent, but the Bible tells us not to swear and not to make promises we aren't prepared to keep. It also shows what to do when we've made a reckless oath.

1. Hasty Vows Cause Pain and Regret

Promises raise expectations. Broken promises break trust and hurt feelings. Consider the unnecessary pain caused by saying, "I'm taking you on a cruise for your birthday," when the birthday comes and work is busy. If we give excuses instead of a trip, we create distance instead of closeness. Broken promises irritate like a splinter under the skin.

A desire to please causes some to make careless promises. But as soon as someone else asks for assistance, they forget the first promise and offer to help the next person. Let's consider how our promises impact those counting on us before we pledge ourselves.

A bride and groom exchange vows before God because marriage is a covenant relationship that should include God (Eccles. 4:12). Separation and divorce take a spiritual, emotional, and financial toll. However, as in other legal arrangements, there are biblical reasons to leave a marriage (1 Cor. 7:10–16; Matt. 19:9).

> Don't make rash promises . . . . When you make a
> promise to God, don't delay in following through, for
> God takes no pleasure in fools. Keep all the promises

you make to him. It is better to say nothing than to make a promise and not keep it. (Eccles. 5:2, 4–5 NLT)

2. Keep Your Vow as unto the Lord (Ps. 50:14) or Use God's Exit
The wise weigh their decisions *before* they pledge. Once we've made a promise, we must either keep it or use God's way out (Ps. 15:1–4).

If you have trapped yourself by your agreement and are caught by what you said—follow my advice and save yourself, for you have placed yourself at your friend's mercy. Now swallow your pride; go and beg to have your name erased. (Prov. 6:2–3 NLT)

My Father's Care

I woke up at 4 a.m. questioning a decision I had made the previous afternoon. I'd told the designer, who'd drawn out a closet plan, we wanted to work with her. In my sleep I had second thoughts.

"Lord, I'm too tired to figure this out. I don't know if we made the right decision. If we jumped too soon, please rescue us." An Old Testament passage came to mind:

If a young woman makes a vow . . . and her father hears of the vow or pledge and does not object to it, then all her vows and pledges will stand. But if her father refuses to let her fulfill the vow or pledge on the day he hears of it, then all her vows and pledges will become invalid. The LORD will forgive her because her father would not let her fulfill them. (Num. 30:3–5 NLT)

I relaxed. I didn't have to figure it out. My Abba would protect me.

I asked the designer to wait until we did more research. She understood. In the end, we chose a different option. If we speak too soon, we can ask our Father what to do.

Despite Jephthah's hasty oath, he showed faith in a time of apostasy. Big mistakes don't have to disqualify us from serving and pleasing God.

Today's Strength Builder

How does viewing God as a stern authoritarian instead of a loving father affect how you treat yourself and others?

CLOSING PRAYER

Use this space to turn your insights and responses into prayers.

Day Four

Samuel—Dedicated to God

Hannah chided herself for dreading their annual trip to Shiloh to worship the Lord. She loved the Lord. But she couldn't suppress the stabbing disappointment—another year of unanswered prayer. Another year childless.

Israel regarded children as God's blessing and infertility as a curse (Deut. 7:13–14; Ps. 127:3–5; Lev. 20:20–21; Jer. 22:30). Hannah certainly felt cursed. Infertility had brought shame and a rival.

When Hannah couldn't produce an heir, her husband Elkanah, like many men in their time, had taken a second wife for the purpose of producing children. Peninnah, the second wife, provoked Hannah "till she wept and would not eat" (1 Sam. 1:7).

Elkanah loved Hannah and couldn't understand why his love wasn't enough. "Hannah, why are you weeping? Why don't you eat? Why are you downhearted? Don't I mean more to you than ten sons?" (1 Sam. 1:8).

After the meal, Hannah stepped away to pray. The bitterness she'd tried to swallow gushed out. "O LORD of Heaven's Armies, if you will look upon my sorrow and answer my prayer and give me a son, then I will give him back to you. He will be yours for his entire lifetime, and as a sign that he has been dedicated to the LORD, his hair will never be cut" (1 Sam. 1:11 NLT).

Hannah wiped her cheeks. She felt clean—and heard.

Do you carry a fear, a stigma, or an unmet longing? Are you ashamed of your status? Let your hurts and longings draw you to God, the giver of every good and perfect gift (James 1:17). When we draw our security and significance from God's gifts instead of from him, the fear of losing or never attaining them consumes our thinking and robs our joy. But when we delight in the Lord, he shapes our desires and opens our hearts to receive his perfect provision (Ps. 37:4–6).

Hannah opened her heart and released her longing. If God gave her a son, that son would serve the Lord all his days. In return, the Lord filled her heart and her womb.

"And the LORD remembered her" (1 Sam. 1:19). She became pregnant and named her son Samuel, "Because I asked the LORD for him" (1 Sam. 1:20).

When the child was weaned, Hannah took him to the Tabernacle in Shiloh. They brought along a three-year-old bull for the sacrifice and a basket of flour and some wine. After sacrificing the bull, they brought the boy to Eli. "Sir, do you remember me?" Hannah asked. "I am the very woman who stood here several

years ago praying to the L ORD. I asked the L ORD to give me this boy, and he has granted my request. Now I am giving him to the L ORD, and he will belong to the L ORD his whole life." And they worshiped the L ORD there.
(1 Sam. 1:24–28 NLT)

Like Moses's mother, Hannah entrusted her son to God by leaving him in the care of another. Samuel would grow up serving God in the Tabernacle under the high priest Eli. Not only were Eli's sons wicked and eventually judged by God, with her history of infertility, Hannah didn't know if she'd have more children. It appears she only saw Samuel once a year after leaving him (1 Sam. 2:19). Yet her prayer expresses only joy (1 Sam. 2:1–11).

Hannah surrendered her deepest longing to God, and God rewarded Hannah with other children. He removed her disgrace and granted her not just any son. Samuel would become Israel's last judge and a mighty prophet of God.

Scripture Reading...
"Then the L ORD sent . . . Jephthah and Samuel, and he delivered you from the hands of your enemies all around you, so that you lived in safety." —1 Samuel 12:11
1 S AMUEL 2:35; 3:1–21

Study and Reflection

1. Eli and his sons served as Israel's priests. Because Eli tolerated his sons' evil behavior, God warned Eli he would take the priesthood away from Eli's family (1 Sam. 2:27–34). Describe the priest God would choose to replace them (1 Sam. 2:35).

2. Samuel was only a boy when he received God's first assignment. What message did God have Samuel deliver (1 Sam. 3:1–15)? What shows this was a difficult assignment?

3. How do we know God was pleased with Samuel (1 Sam. 3:19–21)?

4. Has God ever asked you to deliver a hard message? Why is it important to obey him even when it feels uncomfortable?

5. Record your final thoughts from today's lesson.

Dedicated to Speaking Truth

Would you like God to entrust you with a special message? What if the message made you look judgmental or intolerant? What if delivering it could mean losing your job, your friend—or your life?

Depending on personalities and spiritual gifts, some envision bringing a word of encouragement while others relish Nathan's role of pointing a finger to King David after Uriah's death and saying, "You're the man." A prophet was to deliver God's message, not his own. If the king didn't like the message, he could say, "Off with his head!"

God tapped young Samuel to be his mouthpiece, and he didn't start him off easy. After receiving the message of pending judgment on Eli's household, Samuel "lay down until morning." I doubt he slept since he "was afraid to tell Eli the vision."

I empathize with Samuel. I'd rather encourage someone than deliver a warning. When God has had me give hard feedback or warn people I care about, I've wrestled with those assignments. However, young Samuel showed he would obey God, even in the hard stuff. He hid nothing from Eli. And the Lord was with Samuel and continued to give him messages (1 Sam. 3:19–21).

Those dedicated to truth know that sometimes God has us deliver warnings people will reject, even when they're spoken in humility and for the hearer's good. A wise woman once told me, when I was dreading talking to someone, that if someone is eager to confront, they probably aren't the right messenger. But when someone doesn't want to give the message but God won't let them rest, they probably are his chosen emissary. Her words emboldened me to speak.

Some of my experiences didn't end as I'd hoped. But on more than one occasion, the recipient returned days or years later to acknowledge the message was right. Some even thanked me.

Jephthah dedicated the first thing out of his house. Hannah dedicated her yet-to-be-conceived son to the Lord. God took her gift and turned Samuel into one of Israel's great prophets and priests. Samuel dedicated himself to doing God's will, even when the mission brought pain and danger. God used Samuel to anoint kings and announce judgments.

As God's children, we obey our Father and leave the outcome in his capable hands. Jesus came full of grace and truth (John 1:14). May our words also be seasoned with grace (Col. 4:6). And may we say no more and no less than what he gives us to say (2 Tim. 2:23–26).

Today's Strength Builder

Are you dedicated to wholeheartedly serving the Lord? Practice Samuel's stance: "Here I am, Lord. Use me."

CLOSING PRAYER

Use this space to turn your insights and responses into prayers.

Day Five

Dedicated to Faithfulness

"I will raise up for myself a faithful priest, who will do
according to what is in my heart and mind."
—1 Samuel 2:35

Samuel's sons didn't inherit their father's servant heart. They were greedy, accepted bribes, and perverted justice (1 Sam. 8:3). Samuel's personal heartbreak became public shame when Israel used their dishonesty as an excuse to replace Samuel with a king. Israel's request felt like a slap in the face. Samuel brought his rejection with their request before the Lord.

"Do everything they say to you," the LORD replied, "for they are rejecting me, not you. They don't want me to be their king any longer. Ever since I brought them from Egypt they have continually abandoned me and followed other gods. And now they are giving you the same treatment. Do as they ask, but solemnly

warn them about the way a king will reign over them."
(1 Sam. 8:7–9 NLT)

Samuel delivered God's warning. A king, among other things, would charge exorbitant taxes and press the best of their children into his service. The people refused to listen. Other nations had kings; they wanted a king. God granted their request, and Samuel anointed Saul as Israel's first king.

Saul proved to be a disappointment. He neither listened to nor sought the Lord. God called his halfhearted obedience wholehearted rebellion. When Saul tried to cover his rebellion with a pretense of worship, Samuel delivered the following scathing rebuke before telling him God had torn the kingdom from him and given it to someone better:

> Does the LORD delight in burnt offerings and sacrifices as much as in obeying the LORD? To obey is better than sacrifice, and to heed is better than the fat of rams. For rebellion is like the sin of divination, and arrogance like the evil of idolatry. Because you have rejected the word of the LORD, he has rejected you as king. (1 Sam. 15:22–23)

1 Samuel 15 ends with Samuel mourning for Saul. We pick up our story with God sending Samuel to anoint a new king.

Scripture Reading...
1 SAMUEL 15:35–16:13

Study and Reflection

1. God ruled Israel, and Samuel served as Israel's judge and prophet. The thought of anointing a king repulsed Samuel. But he obeyed God, anointed Saul, and invested in Saul's

success. But Saul proved unfaithful. How did Saul's unrepentance affect Samuel (1 Sam. 15:35)?

2. God told Samuel to stop mourning and move forward. What was Samuel to do (1 Sam. 16:1–5)? What kind of man was God seeking (1 Sam. 13:14)?

3. Based on what God sought in a priest (1 Sam. 2:35) and wanted in a king (1 Sam. 13:14), what qualities matter to God?

4. "Halo effect" describes "the tendency for an impression created in one area [height, appearance] to influence opinion in another area [competence, character]."[9] Contrast the difference between how God and humans evaluate people (1 Sam. 16:6–7). How do you apply this to yourself and the values you impart to your children?

5. We look at David in Chapter Eight. For now, relate God's choosing of David (1 Sam. 16:8–13), Jephthah, Hannah, Samuel, and us with the following:

   Brothers and sisters, think of what you were when you were called. Not many of you were wise by human standards; not many were influential; not many were of noble birth. But God chose the foolish things of the world to shame the wise; God chose the weak things of the world to shame the strong. God chose the lowly things of this world and the despised things—and the

things that are not—to nullify the things that are, so that
no one may boast before him. (1 Cor. 1:26–29)

6. Record your final thoughts from today's lesson.

Dedicated to God—Not a Title

Sometimes we confuse a temporary role in life with our purpose.
It's not unusual for moms to question their identity when their
children leave home. The self-worth of some men dips when they
retire or lose their job.

If the apostle Paul had drawn his value from preaching and
planting churches, imprisonment would have created an identity crisis. But Paul identified himself as a servant of Christ Jesus
(Phil. 1:1). His worth and calling to build God's kingdom didn't
change with his circumstances. He heartily served Christ, whether
preaching to crowds or chained to guards. With that mindset, he
could rejoice when God used his imprisonment to spread the gospel.

Israel noticed Samuel's mounting years and, instead of valu-
ing his faithfulness and wisdom, decided to replace him. Their
rejection of him and of God grieved Samuel. But he set aside his
disappointment, anointed Saul as king, and worked to make his
reign a success.

Despite Samuel's prayers and guidance, Saul would not honor
God. Samuel had known having a king wasn't a good idea, but he'd
done his best by Saul anyway. And Saul had failed. Now Samuel
had to tell Saul God would be unseating him. If Samuel measured
success by what he saw, his effort looked like a waste.

When God sent Samuel to anoint a new king, Samuel held no
delusion. If Saul found out, he would kill him. Yet Samuel obeyed

his Lord. He presented an offering as a covering for his real intent. Jesse's seven sons impressed Samuel, but he relied on God's directions instead of his own inclinations. He refused to dine until he'd completed his mission.

As soon as David entered, the Lord said, "Anoint him; this is the one." I'm sure Samuel expected a stately warrior or at least a grown man, certainly not a ruddy shepherd boy. But he trusted God. The Lord doesn't look for someone who looks the part but for one who looks to him.

Israel rejected Samuel, but God still had work for him. Saul wore the crown, but the Lord confided in and worked through Samuel. God's X-ray eyes pierce through titles and appearances to see the heart. Despite being rejected by Israel, Samuel faithfully prayed for her and served God all his days (1 Sam. 12:23).

Jephthah, Hannah, and Samuel showed dedication to God in different ways, but they all recognized God is worthy of whatever sacrifice obeying him requires. And God remembered them all. Those dedicated to the Lord obey him, no matter the cost.

Today's Strength Builder

King Saul was loved by men and rejected by God. Jephthah, Samuel, and David, who experienced rejection from men, were chosen and commended by God. Live today as one chosen by God and for God.

CLOSING PRAYER

Use this space to turn your insights and responses into prayers.

Prayer Requests

Strength from Conviction

"Finally, a perk," one of the Hebrew youths joked. "We *have* to eat the king's royal food." His companions laughed.

Daniel and his three friends listened to the passing group and eyed each other. "What do we do?" Meshach asked. "We can't eat food offered to idols."

"This is a test," Abednego said. "We know the Babylonians don't follow Moses's dietary laws. The Lord wants us to trust him. But how?"

"A test," Daniel rubbed his chin. "Abednego, that's brilliant! You three ask God for favor while I ask the guard for a different test. Let's see what God does."

⌒

I arrived for jury duty, not knowing what to expect. The clerk called my name with eleven others and directed us to seats in the jury box. One by one, we stated our names, employers, and answered their questions.

"Campus Crusade for Christ." The mention of Christ seemed to send a charge through the courtroom. I had everyone's attention.

In the deliberation room, I contributed my opinion. At lunch, I asked the woman across from me about her necklace.

She covered the engraved pendant with her hand. "Nothing important."

Unable to decipher the cursive script, I ignorantly pressed. She removed her hand, revealing a four-letter curse word. *Way to go, Debbie!*

I sent an arrow prayer and told her that word reminded me of my college days. I'd just begun to walk with the Lord when a friend taught me to replace cussing with thanking God. She stared at me like I was from outer space.

The foreman and I saw the case from opposite perspectives. The jury split evenly between our opposing views. Afterward, he wanted to know more about my faith, and I invited him to my church. Weeks later, he sent a plant with a card that read, "I have a cross around my neck and Jesus in my heart. Thank you."

A coworker once said, "God never commanded the world to go to church. He commanded the church to go to the world." This week we look at four young men who were transported into a world hostile to them and their faith. The kings and cultures that tried to mold them received a bright witness of the living God. But not everyone appreciated them.

Day One
You Can Lead a Boy to Babylon, but You Can't Make Him Drink the Wine

"If you want to do it you'll find a way;
if not you'll find an excuse."
—Roland Peterson[1]

Daniel, Shadrach, Meshach, and Abednego rank among my all-time favorite heroes. Their courage glowed in a dark and desperate time. These young men were probably teenagers in 586 BC when Babylonian armies swept through Jerusalem, destroyed the city, and carried away the third and final deportation of the Jewish people to Babylon.

Jeremiah wrote about the carnage: "Judah has been led away into captivity, oppressed with cruel slavery. She lives among foreign nations and has no place of rest. Her enemies have chased her down, and she has nowhere to turn" (Lam. 1:3 NLT).

The psalmist provides another peek into this horrific time when he looks forward to God repaying Babylon for her cruelty:

> By the rivers of Babylon we sat and wept
>   when we remembered Zion. . . .
> Remember, LORD, what the Edomites did
>   on the day Jerusalem fell.
> "Tear it down," they cried,
>   "tear it down to its foundations!"
> Daughter Babylon, doomed to destruction,
>   happy is the one who repays you
>   according to what you have done to us.
> Happy is the one who seizes your infants
>   and dashes them against the rocks. (Ps. 137:1, 7–9)

Many Jews died by the sword, others by starvation, and thousands more were captured and deported nearly eight hundred miles to Babylon. King Nebuchadnezzar selected Judah's brightest young men to manage his expansive kingdom.

> Then the king ordered Ashpenaz, chief of his court
> officials, to bring into the king's service some of the
> Israelites from the royal family and the nobility—young
> men without any physical defect, handsome, showing

aptitude for every kind of learning, well informed, quick to understand, and qualified to serve in the king's palace. He was to teach them the language and literature of the Babylonians. The king assigned them a daily amount of food and wine from the king's table. They were to be trained for three years, and after that they were to enter the king's service. (Dan. 1:3–5)

King Nebuchadnezzar forced the youths into service and began indoctrinating them in Babylonian culture, religion, and language. In *Thriving in Babylon*, Larry Osborne wrote, "Babylon was also known for its demonic influences. The state-sponsored religion was satanic, and the core curriculum in the schools of higher learning included a large dose of the astrology and the occult."[2]

Nebuchadnezzar changed these men's names from ones that honored some aspect of God to Babylonian names that exalted Babylonian gods. Every time someone spoke their new names, they praised a false god. Daniel, which means "God is my judge," became Belteshazzar, meaning "Bel's prince" (Dan. 1:7). Erwin W. Lutzer writes, "Bel was a title for their demonic god Marduk. It would be like having your name changed to 'Satan's prince.'"[3]

Our enemy, Satan, still targets our brightest and best youth. However, these four Jewish teens show it's not only possible to survive a hostile environment with your faith intact; you can thrive. What was their secret?

Scripture Reading..
"I do not have time to tell about ... the prophets, who ... quenched the fury of the flames." —Hebrews 11:32–34

DANIEL 1

Study and Reflection

1. What stood out to you from today's passage?

2. What do we know about these young men (Dan. 1:3–4, 18–20)?

3. What aspects of these men's lives did this pagan king control (Dan. 1:3–7)? What was he unable to control?

4. Consider an area in your life that's beyond your control. How does the story of Daniel and his friends inspire you in your circumstance?

Conviction Produces Faithfulness

Daniel and his friends lost their homes, families, and even their names. In addition, Nebuchadnezzar most likely had them castrated, fulfilling Isaiah's prophecy and removing any hope of marriage and family (2 Kings 20:17–18; Isa. 39:5–7). "Officials" in Daniel 1:3 is the word for eunuchs.[4] The chief eunuch oversaw Daniel and his companions.

Though we know little about their early years, the actions of these Jewish teenagers reveal deep-rooted faith that held fast through Nebuchadnezzar's turbulent moods and threats. If their parents survived the siege, they would have beamed with pride to hear that their sons stood fast in their faith.

Long before Paul wrote Timothy, "Don't let anyone look down on you because you are young, but set an example for the believers in speech, in conduct, in love, in faith and in purity" (1 Tim. 4:12), Daniel, Shadrach, Meshach, and Abednego practiced this admonition. When the king told them what to eat, they could have reasoned their diet didn't matter now that they lived in Babylon under Nebuchadnezzar. The enticing aroma of barbecued pork and grilled shrimp provided another kind of pressure to comply. But they knew that, according to Mosaic law, the food was unclean and probably came from sacrifices offered to Babylonian gods (Ps. 106:28). Despite everything they'd lost, Daniel, Shadrach, Meshach, and Abednego belonged to God and would honor him by obeying his dietary laws.

Knowing that the chief official, Ashpenaz, was only carrying out the king's orders, Daniel respectfully suggested a ten-day test—a diet of vegetables and water. After ten days, Ashpenaz would compare their appearance with those who ate the king's royal food and decide if they could continue their clean diet. The trial quieted the chief official's legitimate fears of drawing Nebuchadnezzar's ire.

God rewarded these young men with glowing health, combined with superior knowledge and understanding. More importantly, their resolve to not defile themselves bolstered their character for the weightier challenges ahead.

There is no mention that Daniel and his companions tried to coerce the other Jewish young men to join them in following Moses's dietary laws. Instead, they "set an example for the believers in speech, in conduct, in love, in faith and in purity" (1 Tim. 4:12). Though they couldn't control Nebuchadnezzar and their fellow Jews, their convictions—based on their knowledge of God—safely guided Daniel and his friends through the maze of a pagan culture.

Like Daniel, we get thrown into awful circumstances we can't control. We may not be able to stop a spouse from drinking too much, make a child take our concerns seriously, or reverse the progression of an illness. But Scripture provides light for our next step. When we take that step, another will light up. Instead of trying to control what we can't control, we learn to lean on God and practice self-control (Gal. 5:22–23). When we follow God's lead, he does more than we can imagine, and we become strong in battle.

Today's Strength Builder

Consider a predicament you're in. What options do your biblical convictions eliminate? Daniel and his companions found a way to keep their God-given convictions. Ask God to help you with your challenge. Then take the next step.

CLOSING PRAYER

Use this space to turn your insights and responses into prayers.

Day Two
Conviction Produces Stability

God always preserves a faithful remnant. Before Judah's fall, the faithful listened to prophets like Jeremiah plead with Israel to turn from their sin. The remnant prayed and fasted for their nation to return to God. They grieved when Israel flaunted her idolatry. And they suffered with the obstinate when Israel fell to Babylon.

Even though Israel had forsaken God and was delivered over to Nebuchadnezzar, Daniel and his companions knew the Lord stood with them, even in a faraway land (Dan. 1:2, 9, 17). Recalling God's faithfulness to Joseph through slavery and prison (Gen. 39–41) must have encouraged these young men. They would honor the Lord—no matter the cost. They couldn't change their circumstances, but they could trust God and practice self-control.

How Do We Follow Their Example?

James wrote, "Consider it pure joy, my brothers and sisters, whenever you face trials of many kinds, because you know that the testing of your faith produces perseverance. Let perseverance finish its work so that you may be mature and complete, not lacking anything" (James 1:2–4). Trusting God with everyday irritations equips us to stand in hard times.

Engineers test a new bridge before allowing traffic on it. God's tests reveal where our faith is strong and where we need work. Every challenge, big and small, provides an opportunity to flex our faith muscles. The struggle to release injustices and embrace God's promise to work every trial together for good (Rom. 8:28) stretches and strengthens our connection with God.

Scripture Reading..
REVIEW DANIEL 1

Study and Reflection

1. What kind of ruler was Nebuchadnezzar (Dan. 1:10)? What would it be like to work under him?

2. Daniel walked a tightrope. The four wouldn't defile themselves with the king's foods, but neither would they jeopardize Ashpenaz's life. The fruit of the Spirit includes

kindness (Gal. 5:22–23). How did these youths balance these two convictions?

3. What do you learn from Daniel's example? Why did this plan require faith in God?

4. In addition to good health, how else did God reward Daniel, Shadrach, Meshach, and Abednego (Dan. 1:17–20)?

5. What do you learn from these young men to help you live by faith?

6. Record your final thoughts from today's lesson.

How My Dog Helped Me Trust God

My eighty-six-pound poodle, Max, showed me what trust looks like. After being diagnosed with Addison's disease, Max needed to have his blood drawn regularly to check his electrolyte and hormone levels. One week, Max planted himself and refused to go with the technician. I followed the tech, and Max followed me.

I felt like a traitor luring my dog into my vet's lab. I did it to save his life, but Max didn't know that. Did Max think I was heartless to let the vet draw blood from his thin leg month after month?

This made me consider how I trust God when I am hurting. It's easy to believe that if I understood the purpose of my pain, I'd trust him better. But is that true?

Imagine explaining Max's condition to him. I could read him the symptoms off the Internet. I could show him his lab reports. I could remind him how he almost died. But would that help Max have his blood drawn?

My knowledge concerning the treatment of Max's illness surpasses his. I know the brief pain of the needle produces lasting benefits. Sometimes God allows us to see the benefit of our losses. But many of our *whys* remain unanswered.

Isaiah 55:8–9 offers some understanding:

"For my thoughts are not your thoughts, neither are your ways my ways," declares the LORD. "As the heavens are higher than the earth, so are my ways higher than your ways and my thoughts than your thoughts."

The difference between my thoughts and my dog's is much less than the distance between God's thoughts and mine. If Max can't understand why I have his blood drawn, do I think I can understand why God lets pain touch me?

But God has not left me without assurance. He promised:

- "For our present troubles are small and won't last very long. Yet they produce for us a glory that vastly outweighs them and will last forever!" (2 Cor. 4:17 NLT).
- "Yet what we suffer now is nothing compared to the glory he will reveal to us later" (Rom. 8:18 NLT).

A child of God can't lose a hair without God noticing. Perhaps Romans 8:31 sums up all we really need to remember. "If God is for us, who can be against us?"

Life on this planet is a vapor. But how we live echoes through eternity. Pain, loss, and confusion provide opportunities to trust the Master. The pain you, Max, and I experience is as real as the losses suffered by Daniel, Shadrach, Meshach, and Abednego. But the pain is temporary. God sees the big picture and promises to work the wrongs and injustices that touch us together for our eternal good (Rom. 8:28).

Max didn't trust the vet tech, but he trusted me. Jesus didn't trust men, but he trusted his Father. Daniel and his companions couldn't trust Nebuchadnezzar, but they trusted God. So can we.

Will you trust the one who shed his blood for you? When he allows pain to touch you, he promises to use even this for your eternal good and to walk with you through your trials (Isa. 43:1–3).

When I see Max romp across the yard without a symptom of Addison's, I thank God for blood tests and shots. I remember how sick he was without them. Max doesn't understand the connection. He doesn't need to. He only needs to know I take care of him.

Daniel and his friends sailed through their first tests. God rewarded them with glowing health, high IQs (intelligence quotients), and excellent SIQs (spiritual intelligence quotients). The next test will come with higher stakes—comply or die.

Today's Strength Builder

What loss still pains you? Ask God to help you move your focus off the whys onto the one who loves you.

CLOSING PRAYER

Use this space to turn your insights and responses into prayers.

Day Three

When Convictions Come under Fire

"[Who] quenched the fury of the flames."
—Hebrews 11:34

How do you respond when the world you know and trust flips upside down and the wicked land on top? Retreat? Lash out? Or stand steadfast?

We can only imagine the horrors Daniel, Shadrach, Meshach, and Abednego witnessed when the Babylonian army herded the Hebrews to Babylon. What happened to their families? If raiders dashed Israel's babies against the rocks, what did they do to the sick and elderly? Instead of curling into a fetal position or melding into their new culture, the fabulous four honored God and served this unrighteous ruler by practicing Jeremiah 29:7: "Seek the peace and prosperity of the city to which I have carried you into exile. Pray to the Lord for it, because if it prospers, you too will prosper."

When King Nebuchadnezzar threatened to kill his wise men, including Daniel, Shadrach, Meshach, and Abednego, God provided Daniel with the interpretation of Nebuchadnezzar's dream (Dan. 2). This saved the lives of all the king's wise men. King Nebuchadnezzar, amazed that any god could convey such knowledge, proclaimed, "Surely your God is the God of gods and the Lord of kings and a revealer of mysteries, for you were able to reveal this mystery" (Dan. 2:47).

But his gratitude was short-lived. Jealous peers and the king's ego soon threw the four Hebrews into another crisis.

Shadrach, Meshach, and Abednego lived and worked among brutal men who envied their successes. When King Nebuchadnezzar erected a golden idol and promised death to anyone who refused to bow before it, some of the wise men (astrologers) approached King Nebuchadnezzar. "There are some Jews whom you have set over the affairs of the province of Babylon—Shadrach, Meshach and Abednego—who pay no attention to you, Your Majesty. They neither serve your gods nor worship the image of gold you have set up" (Dan. 3:12).

Bow before an idol or be thrown into a fiery furnace. It would be easy to cave under such heat (pun intended). But when the king's demands opposed the King of king's commands, these Hebrews stood by their convictions: God before king; God before personal safety; God first.

Our convictions guide us when we're under fire. If we live to love God with all our heart, soul, mind, and strength, nobody can block that goal. And as difficult as it may be to believe, ruthless people can't stop God's plans for our lives (Ps. 37:17, 23). Some who observe your faith under pressure will see Christ.

Daniel, Shadrach, Meshach, and Abednego's fortitude gave God an opportunity to shine before pagan leaders in high places. God may place us in hostile settings to display his glory to people who scoff at our faith. A good friend, whom I'll call Laura, experienced this when she tried to reach some professional associates by joining their group for lunch.

Faith under Fire

When the conversation mocked biblical values, Laura wondered, *What am I doing here?*

She examined the faces of the successful people surrounding her and realized no one in the room probably shared her views. She prayed for words of wisdom. None came. She bit back the retorts that rose to counter their tasteless remarks.

When the conversation jumped to a new topic, the woman at her elbow said, "This has been fun. Let's do it again." Laura realized God had answered her prayer. He'd called her to win hearts, not arguments. He wanted her to love these women. "I'll host next time," she offered.

God used opposition to clarify my friend's commitment. The threat of death strengthened Shadrach, Meshach, and Abednego's resolve to live for God. Because they chose God, Nebuchadnezzar received a rare revelation of One more precious than his golden idol.

Are you living for something—Someone—bigger than yourself? How many reside in heaven today because of the courage of people like Laura, Shadrach, Meshach, and Abednego?

Scripture Reading..

DANIEL 2:47–3:30

Study and Reflection

1. Write your observations from today's passage.

2. "So at the sound of the musical instruments, all the people, whatever their race or nation or language, bowed to the ground and worshiped the gold statue that King Nebuchadnezzar had set up" (Dan. 3:7 NLT). The astrologers that came forth to accuse Shadrach, Meshach, and Abednego probably served under these Hebrew men (Dan. 2:49). Bringing this to the king's attention would force these Hebrews to either deny their faith or be thrown into the furnace (Dan. 3:11). How did Shadrach, Meshach, and

Abednego's convictions about God govern their actions
(Dan. 3:13–18, 28)?

3. What do you learn from their example?

4. Name the special blessings that came from this trial
   (Dan. 3:25–30).

5. Think of the trials the Lord has brought you through. Did you
   experience Jesus more closely in your furnace? If so, how?

6. What do you learn about God? How do you apply this story
   to your life?

Moving from "What If" to "Even If"

My husband and I led a small group of parents who wanted to live
for Christ. A man from the Netherlands recalled stories of how
the Nazis tortured those who resisted Hitler's ideals. Nightmares
of caving before cruel interrogators and denying Christ tormented
him. Would he deny his Lord under such pressure? Reading of
Shadrach, Meshach, and Abednego's courage raised the same concern in me. Would I stand true in similar circumstances?

Paul wrote, "Not that we are adequate in ourselves *so as* to consider anything as *having come* from ourselves, but our adequacy is
from God" (2 Cor. 3:5 NASB—emphasis in original). Paul remained

faithful through martyrdom. His confidence was in Christ, not in himself.

Jesus told his disciples, "But when you are arrested and stand trial, don't worry in advance about what to say. Just say what God tells you at that time, for it is not you who will be speaking, but the Holy Spirit" (Mark 13:11 NLT). I believe Shadrach, Meshach, and Abednego said exactly what the Holy Spirit inspired them to say in that moment.

Music and Threats

Nebuchadnezzar knew the power of music. Patriotic tunes rouse people to their feet. Music lifts spirits or pulls them down. Some melodies lull us into a false sense of security, leaving us vulnerable to dangerous influences. Nebuchadnezzar used music to seduce the people into compliance. If that didn't work, surely the threat of painful death would.

When some astrologers ratted on Shadrach, Meshach, and Abednego, Nebuchadnezzar flew into a rage and summoned the three Jews. When they saw this red-faced tyrant who couldn't control even his own temper, I can't imagine what they felt. But their response to Nebuchadnezzar's threat rang out like Gideon's trumpet.

> "I will give you one more chance to bow down . . . .
> But if you refuse, you will be thrown immediately into
> the blazing furnace. And then what god will be able to
> rescue you from my power?"
> Shadrach, Meshach, and Abednego replied, "O
> Nebuchadnezzar, we do not need to defend ourselves
> before you. If we are thrown into the blazing furnace,
> the God whom we serve is able to save us. He will
> rescue us from your power, Your Majesty. But even if he

doesn't, we want to make it clear to you, Your Majesty,
that we will never serve your gods or worship the gold
statue you have set up." (Dan. 3:15–18 NLT)

Angels cheered, and Nebuchadnezzar exploded.

> And [Nebuchadnezzar] commanded some of the
> strongest soldiers in his army to tie up Shadrach,
> Meshach and Abednego and throw them into the
> blazing furnace. . . . The furnace [was] so hot that
> the flames of the fire killed the soldiers who took up
> Shadrach, Meshach and Abednego. (Dan. 3:20, 22)

Shadrach, Meshach, and Abednego declared, "Our God is able
to save us." They knew the power of their God. They also knew his
ways are beyond understanding. His eternal viewpoint meant he
never made a mistake. He was worthy of their allegiance even if he
didn't rescue them. He was good even when bad things happened.
They would remain faithful *even if* God let them die.

I hope I never have to face a "do or die" command. But Shadrach,
Meshach, and Abednego set an example I want to follow in everyday
challenges as well as dire situations.

What Can We Learn from Their Example?

Shadrach, Meshach, and Abednego faced big problems, yet they
didn't entertain negative *what if* thinking. "What if God doesn't save
us?" "What if I can't bear the pain of the flames?" What negative
what if thoughts tend to sap your strength?

- *What if* this illness won't heal?
- *What if* my child continues into a destructive lifestyle?
- *What if* I fail?
- *What if* the worst happens?

Instead of focusing on *what if*s, Shadrach, Meshach, and Abednego declared *even if* faith. We can too.

- *Even if* the worst happens, I will trust God's goodness.
- *Even if* I mess up, God will work it together for good.
- *Even if* my child goes astray, God seeks prodigals.
- *Even if* this ends in death, Jesus is the resurrection and the life.

Declarations of *even if* faith dissolve fears like water melted the wicked witch in Oz.

The sun is more than one hundred times bigger than the earth. Yet I can block out the sun by holding a small pebble over my eye. God is much bigger than the sun. But obsessing over my problems blocks my vision of him.

When our God is small, our problems are huge. But no problem can stand before a big God.

And what happened to those who bowed before Nebuchadnezzar's idol? The furnace killed some of the king's strongest soldiers as they threw the three men in. Security is never found in bowing before tyrants. It is found in a Big God.

Today's Strength Builder

List some faith-filled *even if*s you can declare when strength-sapping *what if*s taunt you.

CLOSING PRAYER

Use this space to turn your insights and responses into prayers.

Day Four

Live by Faith; Lead by Example

*"You have enemies? Why, it is the story of every man who
has done a great deed or created a new idea. It is the
cloud which thunders around everything which shines."*
—Victor Hugo[5]

We love the story of Daniel in the lions' den. Did you know Daniel
was probably in his eighties when he faced the lions? Many years
and a few kings have passed between teenage Daniel's export into
Babylon and his night in the lions' den.

The Bible says, "Everyone who does evil hates the light"
(John 3:20). Those in leadership with Daniel schemed against this
godly man who excelled in everything. Daniel faithfully served
his God and king, so the only way to trap him was to ban the
practice of his faith.

Daniel's enemies knew he prayed three times a day. They flat-
tered King Darius into signing an irrevocable law to trap his favorite
administrator. The new law made it illegal to pray to anyone other
than Darius for thirty days. Anyone who dared to violate this decree
would be thrown into the lions' den.

Peter could have been remembering Daniel when he wrote,
"For it is better, if it is God's will, to suffer for doing good than for
doing evil" (1 Pet. 3:17). When Daniel learned about the decree,
despite the threat of the lions' den, he headed home and knelt before
his open window to thank God and ask for help. No Jewish law
commanded one to pray before an open window. He could have
prayed under his bed covers at night for thirty days. But Daniel's
custom and personal conviction guided him.

Daniel practiced Philippians 4:6–7: "Do not be anxious about
anything, but in every situation, by prayer and petition, with
thanksgiving, present your requests to God. And the peace of

God, which transcends all understanding, will guard your hearts and your minds in Christ Jesus." The very disciplines his enemies targeted carried him through this new trial. But did God answer his prayer?

Scripture Reading...
"And what more shall I say? I do not have time to tell about . . . the prophets, . . . who shut the mouths of lions." —Hebrews 11:32-34

DANIEL 6

Study and Reflection

1. Why did the other leaders hate Daniel enough to plot his death (Dan. 6:1–5)?

2. It's rare to find faithful men and women in any area of life; yet Daniel shows it's possible to live a blameless life even in a corrupt political arena (Dan. 6:4). It isn't clear how many of the 122 leaders actively plotted to destroy Daniel. No one seems to have spoken against the scheme. What does this reveal about Daniel's life in exile?

3. What did Daniel do when he learned of the decree that targeted him (Dan. 6:6–11)?

4. According to the law of the Medes and the Persians, no one, including the king, could undo a decree once it was signed into law. After the king's failed attempts to rescue

Daniel, what did he recognize to be Daniel's only hope (Dan. 6:12–16)?

5. After sixty-six years in Babylon, Daniel was still known as "one of the exiles from Judah." He faithfully served the various kings but never considered Babylon his home. God commended the patriarchs and Moses for living as strangers on earth and longing for a heavenly home (Heb. 11:13–16, 26). Because our citizenship is in heaven (Phil. 3:20), 1 Peter 2:11 calls us foreigners and exiles, too. How do you protect yourself from becoming enmeshed in the world?

6. Who spent the worst night: King Darius or Daniel? How and why did God rescue Daniel (Dan. 6:17–22)?

7. What happened to Daniel's enemies, the king, and Daniel (Dan. 6:23–28)?

8. Record your final thoughts from today's lesson.

Four Brave Men, Two Pompous Kings, and One Awesome God

Shadrach, Meshach, and Abednego were probably in their early twenties when the king tried to roast them in the furnace. In his eighties, Daniel surely felt too old for an overnight pajama party with lions. Yet God was at work in both injustices.

The fire meant to destroy Shadrach, Meshach, and Abednego killed the men who manhandled them and showcased the Son of God. The lions didn't touch Daniel but crushed the evil schemers before they hit the ground. Living a godly life didn't spare the faithful from danger or being hated. Yet God stood with them through their danger.

The four men's dogged determination to honor God, even when they didn't know whether God would save them, inspires us in dark times.

- As Romans 13:1 instructs, these men cooperated with governing authorities in areas that didn't violate their consciences before God. But when human laws contradicted God's laws, they obeyed God (Dan. 6:22).
- They served their king but worshiped only God (Exod. 20:3; Deut. 5:9). Putting God first protected them from their enemies' traps (Dan. 3:28; Deut. 8:19).
- Like the patriarchs before them, they lived as strangers in this world (Heb. 11:9, 13, 16; Dan. 6:10).
- They let God defend them and his name (Dan. 3:16–17; 6:21–22).
- They experienced a special revelation of and closeness with Christ (Phil. 3:10). Shadrach, Meshach, and Abednego strolled through a fire with the preincarnate Christ (Dan. 3:25). Daniel spent a whole night with an angel (Dan. 6:22).
- Their lives glorified God (Dan. 3:28–29, 6:26–27).
- God honored them (Dan. 3:30, 6:28).

Daniel, Shadrach, Meshach, and Abednego sought neither conflict nor attention. They simply honored God by knowing and practicing his ways. If we could ask them, "Was it worth it to follow the Lord," I have no doubt they would say, "Yes, yes, yes!"

While God did not insulate them from difficulties, he carried them through their troubles. The fellowship of sufferings turned bitter trials into sweet closeness with the Lord and with each other. Daniel and his friends modeled faith in life and in facing death. "They did not love their lives so much as to shrink from death" (Rev. 12:11).

One day Christ will take us home, and we'll receive all he's promised. Until then, may we live with the courage of Daniel, Shadrach, Meshach, and Abednego.

> *Even if* [God] does not [rescue us], . . . we will not serve your gods or worship the image of gold you have set up. (Dan. 3:18—emphasis added)

Today's Strength Builder

What habits keep you grounded in eternal truth?

CLOSING PRAYER

Use this space to turn your insights and responses into prayers.

Day Five
"Even If" Convictions

*Frodo: "I wish the Ring had never come to me.
I wish none of this had happened."*

*Gandalf: "So do all who live to see such times,
but that is not for them to decide. All we have to
decide is what to do with the time that is given to us."*
—J. R. R. Tolkien, *The Lord of the Rings*

My husband and I zipped along I-95 South, heading home from the DC area on a section of interstate that never sleeps. Occasionally, wannabe race car drivers cut in and out too close for comfort. I marveled at how a tight space could hold so many speeding vehicles. Suddenly traffic slowed. "Warning: Unmarked Pavement Ahead."

Without painted lines to delineate the last two lanes, the space that had held four lanes of speeding traffic shrank to three lanes of tentative driving. My shoulders tensed, watching vehicles gauge where to move. The markings that limited the space of each car also increased everyone's speed and safety. I shuddered to imagine I-95 without marked lanes. Then I thought of our culture.

In the name of tolerance and personal freedom, we've erased the moral boundaries that protect us from being broadsided as we navigate life (Prov. 8:36; 14:12). Our children suffer the result. When . . .

- Those who speak truth are canceled,
- Dishonest greed is praised as business savvy,
- Immorality is celebrated as personal expression,
- Facts are twisted to promote political narratives,
- Vile language and pornographic images are protected as freedom of speech,
- References to God and morality are censored as separation of church and state,
- Human life is viewed as less valuable than an eagle's egg,

. . . then we are neither free nor safe. Predators use cyberspace to slip through the walls of our homes like a Trojan horse and seduce our children. Those who refuse to cower are targeted and persecuted.

Timeless parameters guard us against waffling emotions and false narratives. They protect us from needless crashes and heartaches and provide stability to individuals, families, and nations. They steer us away from the pitfalls those who cross the lines will encounter. While cultural forces try to erase the moral lines that define right and wrong, true right and wrong never change.

Like the solid and broken lines on an interstate, biblical principles clarify which lines to never cross from the disputable matters that can be negotiated with care. For example, no idol worship is a solid line. However, in the early church, Paul called eating foods associated with idol worship a disputable matter.

While believers shared the biblical absolute—worship only God—their personal convictions varied on whether food offered to idols applied. Some, including Paul, ate meat offered to idols. Others couldn't disassociate the meat from the idolatry they'd left. Paul addressed those differences in Romans 14, concluding with, "Blessed is the one who does not condemn himself by what he approves" (Rom. 14:22).

A conviction is a firm belief. It can be based on a law or promise from Scripture, or it can be a thought-out resolution between God and us. Daniel's personal conviction, not a biblical law, compelled him to bow before an open window three times a day.

Just as pavement lines protect us from being sideswiped or hit head-on, personal convictions protect us from cultural pitfalls and personal weaknesses. They help us stay true to our Lord when the world pressures us to conform. Spiritual gifts and individual histories influence the personal convictions we need to establish.

Certain music, people, or settings that tempt one person to feel sadness, lust, or rage may have no influence on someone else. To force others to live by our personal convictions is legalism. As we become aware of our vulnerabilities, we "make no provision for the flesh" (Rom. 13:11–14 NASB). Cults tell their followers how to think, dress, and act. But "where the Spirit of the Lord is, there is freedom" (2 Cor. 3:17).

Satan's tentacles infiltrate the medical, religious, political, business, educational, and entertainment arenas. Personal convictions based on biblical wisdom provide clear lines to lead us through the chaos called worldly enlightenment.

Would you like one clear guiding principle? Ask God to provide a scripture for your situation. Remember all God-pleasing convictions include love as God defines it (1 Cor. 13:4–7). Godly love fulfills the requirements of God's law (Mark 12:29–31; Rom. 13:8).

Love for God and kindness to others shaped Daniel, Shadrach, Meshach, and Abednego's choices and kept them in the lane of God's favor. Staying within the lines of biblical truth keeps us on track when the pressures of the world and our emotions threaten to wreck us.

Scripture Reading...
Highlights from Daniel chapters 1, 3, and 6
"Everyone who acknowledges me publicly here on earth, I will also acknowledge before my Father in heaven. But everyone who denies me here on earth, I will also deny before my Father in heaven." —Matthew 10:32–33 (NLT)

"For our present troubles are small and won't last very long. Yet they produce for us a glory that vastly outweighs them and will last forever!" —2 Cor. 4:17 (NLT)

HEBREWS 11:35–38

Study and Reflection

1. What personal conviction caused Daniel to ask permission not to eat the food nor drink the wine from the king's table (Dan. 1:8)?

2. List some convictions one might have based on the following scriptures and the four Hebrews' example. "Don't you realize that your body is the temple of the Holy Spirit, who lives in you and was given to you by God? You do not belong to yourself, for God bought you with a high price. So you must honor God with your body" (1 Cor. 6:19–20 NLT). "You can be sure that no immoral, impure, or greedy person will inherit the Kingdom of Christ and of God. For a greedy person is an idolater, worshiping the things of this world" (Eph. 5:5 NLT).

3. How did God reward the four (Dan. 1:17)? How has God rewarded you when you honored him? (This could be an internal reward.)

4. What was Nebuchadnezzar asking the three Hebrews to do, and what was the cost of refusal (Dan. 3:14–15)?

5. How does an eternal perspective protect us from the pressures in our world (Matt. 10:22–32; 2 Cor. 4:17)?

6. What habit had Daniel established that his enemies used against him (Dan. 6:4–13)? How did that habit contribute to his rescue (Dan. 6:19–23)?

7. As mentioned earlier, Daniel could have prayed under the covers and broken no biblical law. Yet Daniel was willing to go to the lions' den for this personal conviction. An Arizona therapist lost his license when he helped a youth no one else had been able to help. What unauthorized therapy had he added? Prayer. What personal convictions do you hold that you are unwilling to compromise—no matter the cost?

8. God didn't spare the faithful four from human wrath, but he showed up in the furnace and sent an angel into the lions' den. But not all faith stories turn out in this life as we hope. All but one of the apostles were martyred. Hebrews 11:35–38 describes what some believers suffered for Christ. What epitaph does verse 38 give?

9. Record your final thoughts from today's lesson.

Unanswered Prayer

Do you feel like God's stepchild when your prayers go unanswered? Surely Daniel and his buddies prayed for help when Nebuchadnezzar conquered Israel, yet they were captured, castrated, and pressed into the king's service. Their lives appeared to rest on the capricious whims of an egotistical ruler.

Sometimes God doesn't answer our prayers like we want. However, those unanswered prayers often become our favorite stories because, in the furnace of affliction surrounded by snarling beasts, we experience the sweetness of Jesus.

Perhaps, like Jesus, Daniel asked for the cup of suffering to be removed. God heard Daniel's prayer, but he didn't keep Daniel from facing the lions. He did something better. He sent an angel to close the lions' mouths.

Often our unanswered prayers make the best stories. When God doesn't answer your prayer as you hoped, don't give up hope. You may just be part of a bigger story.

Wisdom at Work

Richard Wurmbrand, a pastor in communist Romania, was no stranger to torture and imprisonment. Suffering for his faith influenced how he presented Christ to young people. Wurmbrand took children to the lion exhibit at the zoo. Instead of promising happiness, he explained how Rome threw early Christians to the lions. Many of these children's parents had suffered or were suffering imprisonment for their faith.

"Knowing the cost, who will commit to following Christ?" he asked.

Eyes glistened as each one counted the cost before stepping forward.

We live in a culture that has become increasingly hostile to believers. Many in government, business, and education seek to remove those who practice biblical values. Jesus said the world would hate his followers. Do you have what it takes to follow Christ? Do I?

The wisdom that guided Daniel and his friends through a pagan culture filled with deadly snares came from their commitment to follow the Lord, no matter the cost. When we put God first, he supplies the strength and wisdom we need (James 1:2–8).

The four Hebrews didn't enjoy a democracy with free speech. They couldn't picket the king's table or send out petitions to have Nebuchadnezzar's idol removed. Personal holiness was their superpower. These young men learned Babylonian history, religion, and language. They answered to pagan names. They faithfully served idolatrous kings. But they refused to eat the king's food, worship idols, or stop praying to the true God.

Daniel, Shadrach, Meshach, and Abednego could have reasoned it would be better to live and use their influence for good. Would it hurt to outwardly comply if they worshiped God in their hearts?

But their convictions said otherwise. Outward compliance affects the inner core. To bow before the idol was to deny the preeminence of God. No one can serve two masters. They couldn't serve Nebuchadnezzar's gods and the Lord. Following their convictions landed the three in a fiery furnace and Daniel in a lions' den. It also put them in the Bible's Hall of Faith (Heb. 11:33–34).

When the preincarnate Christ appeared in the furnace, the three young men probably assumed he'd come to usher them into heaven. An eternal perspective promised that any years lost on earth would be spent in heaven enjoying real life (2 Cor. 5:6–8).

Challenging times shaped their stories. Just as God raised them up, he's appointed you and me for this time. Perhaps now more than ever, we must decide to follow Jesus. No turning back. No turning back.

Today's Strength Builder

Returning to our opening analogy, are there some dotted-line convictions that need to become solid lines? Align your convictions with biblical truth and seek friendships with those who share your biblical values.

CLOSING PRAYER

Use this space to turn your insights and responses into prayers.

Prayer Requests

_____

_____

_____

_____

_____

_____

_____

_____

_____

_____

_____

_____

_____

_____

_____

Strength in the Lord and His Armor

"YOUR MAJESTY, SOMEONE'S STEPPED UP TO FIGHT THE giant," King Saul's attendant said.

"Well, bring him here. Quick, man. What are you waiting for?" King Saul paced inside his tent. The smell of fear had filled the camp over the past forty days. He needed a miracle—yesterday. Could this man turn things around?

The tent flap rustled. "Your Majesty, here's the one I spoke of."

King Saul gawked at the youth who stood before him. Was this a joke? "Why," he stammered, "you're so . . . young. You can't fight this Philistine; he's been a warrior from his youth."

Day One
How to Kill a Giant

"The true soldier fights not because he hates what is in front of him, but because he loves what is behind him."
—G. K. Chesterton[1]

One look at my son, and I knew he'd had a terrible day. At lunch, when opening a ketchup packet, some squirted across the table and splattered a fellow kindergartener. She yelled at him, drawing attention to my self-conscious introvert. He turned aside to hide his embarrassment.

We'd moved to our fourth state in four years. Our children slept on floor mattresses while we waited for our house to be finished and the rest of our belongings to arrive. My son's distress wrenched my heart. I wanted to protect him, but I couldn't tag along at school.

After tucking him into bed that night, God reminded me of David and Goliath. As a youth, David faced a giant warrior who intimidated an army of seasoned soldiers. Where did he find his courage?

David grew strong defending his father's sheep from wild beasts. God's Word reframed my thinking. My son needed faith and courage, not insulation.

At breakfast, I reminded Brant of David and Goliath. "You don't go to school alone," I said. "The Lord, who was with David, goes with you."

I don't know which encouraged Brant more, the story of David or my new attitude. He straightened his small shoulders and left, ready to face the day—in the strength of the Lord.

David and Goliath

Even young children thrill at the story of David and Goliath. God selected David—the youngest of eight sons, overlooked by his family and doubted by his king—to slay an intimidating giant and reign as Israel's second king. God's own Son would come from David's line and sit on a heavenly throne.

Righteous indignation burned in David as he listened to the nearly ten-foot Philistine taunt God's army. "I defy the armies of Israel today! Send me a man who will fight me!" (1 Sam. 17:10 NLT).

Years of watching sheep had taught David to trust God's invisible presence. The Lord who'd used him to defeat bears and lions didn't shrink before giants. If nations were but a drop in the bucket to God (Isa. 40:15), what was one large man?

The day my kindergartener came home in distress, David's faith quieted my overprotective maternal instinct. Remembering the size of my God changed my focus, strengthened my son, and restored our peace.

Training our children to walk in God's strength protects them from evils worse than sword-swinging giants.

Scripture Reading..
1 SAMUEL 17

Study and Reflection

1. "Whoever can be trusted with very little can also be trusted with much" (Luke 16:10). How did David demonstrate trust-worthiness before he faced Goliath (1 Sam. 17:14–22)?

2. Why did David volunteer to fight the Philistine that terrified Israel's whole camp (1 Sam. 17:26, 36–37)?

3. David faced discouraging messages from "his side" *before* facing Goliath (1 Sam. 17:28–30, 33–39). He apparently had already learned how to strengthen himself in the Lord (1 Sam. 30:6). Apply this to your life.

4. Have you ever been pressured to fit a certain mold? The other moms enjoy crafts. The other speakers are tech

whizzes. Or your friends know how you should train your special needs child. David faced Goliath in God's strength, but he also faced him *as David*, the shepherd boy anointed to be king—not as a soldier in Saul's armor. How do you apply this when people dictate how you should fight your battles?

5. Contrast how David and Goliath showed up to fight (1 Sam. 17:4–7, 37–47).

6. What do you learn from David to help you live strong?

7. Record your final thoughts from today's lesson.

On Whose Name Will You Focus?

When a sonogram and follow-up MRI revealed a dirty mass inside me, I couldn't ignore this interruption. My unwelcome guest grew ten feet when my doctor referred me to an oncologist. Both my parents and father-in-law died of cancer. My stomach twisted when I pictured entering the towering UNC Cancer Center—as a patient.

Some loved ones urged me to hasten my surgery. "We need to know if it's cancer. If so, what stage?"

I understood. If we know our giant's name, we know what we're up against. My giant led me to David and Goliath.

As [David] was talking with them, Goliath, the Philistine champion from Gath, stepped out from his lines and shouted his usual defiance, and David heard it.

Whenever the Israelites saw the man, they all fled from him in great fear. (1 Sam. 17:23–24)

To better appreciate this scene, let's look at the players. According to Numbers 1:3, men twenty or older could serve in Israel's army. If four of David's older brothers weren't old enough to serve and if these brothers were a year apart, David would have been around fifteen when his father sent him to check on his older brothers at war.

This Philistine champion towered a good three and a half feet over the average soldier. No one, not David's older brothers nor Israel's accomplished military king, would face him. But the brute that sent an army fleeing only roused David's indignation. "Who is this uncircumcised Philistine that he should defy the armies of the living God?" (1 Sam. 17:26).

King Saul heard about David and sent for him. His hopes collapsed when he met this rosy-cheeked youth. David's older brother had already accused him of selfishness. Failure meant certain death. David lacked the status of an army private. If victory depended on age, size, title, weapons, birth order, or experience, David was done before he'd begun. Yet, David didn't hesitate.

David didn't focus on his critics or his limitations. He dismissed his brother's derision, addressed his king's concerns, and *focused on the Lord*. While Israel's soldiers compared Goliath to themselves, David compared the giant to God. Next to Israel's God, Goliath was a cockroach to be squashed.

The heart of a warrior king beat strong inside David. "The Lord who rescued me from the paw of the lion and the paw of the bear will rescue me from the hand of this Philistine" (1 Sam. 17:37). Defending sheep had taught David how to be strong in the Lord and prepared him to be God's instrument in this battle between good and evil.

Goliath, armed with a sword, spear, and javelin, ranted as he paced the battlefield. His shield bearer scurried to keep in step. Unhurried by the giant's threats, David selected five smooth stones from a stream. Armed with his sling and shepherd's staff, he crossed the valley to face this snarling killer.

> You come against me with sword and spear and javelin, but I come against you in the name of the LORD Almighty, the God of the armies of Israel, whom you have defied. This day the Lord will deliver you into my hands, and I'll strike you down and cut off your head. This very day I will give the carcasses of the Philistine army to the birds and the wild animals, and the whole world will know that there is a God in Israel. All those gathered here will know that it is not by sword or spear that the LORD saves; for the battle is the LORD's, and he will give all of you into our hands. (1 Sam. 17:45–47)

The story of how David triumphed over Goliath changed how I waited for surgery. David didn't bother to even say Goliath's name. The only name that mattered was the name of the Lord Almighty.

If surgery revealed a giant named cancer, it didn't change God. The Lord Almighty is bigger than cancer. If my illness ended in death, it didn't change God. Jesus is "the resurrection and the life" (John 11:25).

My son said, "Mom, you're more peaceful over this than over everyday troubles." That wasn't a compliment! But he was right. I couldn't fight this in my strength. I had to focus on the name of the Lord. In return, he swathed me in peace.

I'm thankful my mass was benign. I'm also grateful God used this to teach me again the importance of focusing on the name of the Lord. How much peace do we forfeit by focusing on our problems instead of on him? Neither my weakness nor my enemy's strength changes God. But the wrong focus steals my peace and strength. David's hope didn't rest in his weapons, himself, or the size of his giant. Ours shouldn't either.

Perhaps you're facing a giant with an intimidating name and history—a giant named Debt, Death, Infertility, Injustice, Adultery, Divorce, Cancer, Diabetes, COVID, or Learning Disability. Human strength is no match for your monster. On what name will you focus—the name of your giant or your God? When our God is small, every problem feels big. But giants tumble before a big God.

Today's Strength Builder

Choose to focus on the name of your God instead of your problem.

CLOSING PRAYER

Use this space to turn your insights and responses into prayers.

Strength from Discernment

What if I told you the devil wants to use you to accomplish his schemes? At a women's luncheon, I asked my Christian audience if they ever experienced accusations and taunts after leaving Bible study. Hands shot up throughout the room.

Are you aware that the world, the flesh, and the devil plant ideas in your head? Did you know the devil uses people—including believers—to steal, kill, and destroy what's good and lovely?

My cousin led a strong prison ministry where inmates were coming to Christ and being baptized. Another denomination complained to the prison chaplain about this denomination's method of baptism. Their whining got both groups expelled.

Jesus said, "My sheep listen to my voice; I know them, and they follow me" (John 10:27). Can you distinguish the Lord's voice from other voices?

Professionals learn to identify counterfeit money by studying real money. The better we know Jesus, the quicker we spot Satan's tricks. While we focus primarily on Christ, we must recognize the enemy's schemes (2 Cor. 2:11).

How to Recognize Your Enemy's Schemes

An email said my friend was stranded in England. Someone had stolen her wallet and passport. She needed money ASAP. The email address belonged to my friend, but the tone didn't.

Days later, my friend emailed to say someone had hacked her account. "Don't send money. I'm not overseas."

Knowing scammers prey on the unsuspecting puts us on guard. We need the same wariness in reviewing our thoughts.

Many years ago, Francis Schaeffer presented a news clip that led you to believe you'd witnessed police brutality. After stirring our emotions, he showed the same scenario, this time from the beginning. What first looked like gross injustice now revealed self-defense. If we're not careful, our enemy will stir us into believing his scams.[2]

Satan would have us confuse righteous indignation, which motivated David to risk his life to face Goliath, with personal resentment that pursues retaliation when someone hurts our pride. The devil wants to sabotage our trust in God, so he magnifies our lowest moments and erases from our memory the many times God protected us. How do we keep from being conned? Here's help.

Satan Intends Destruction

"The thief comes *only* to steal and kill and destroy" (John 10:10—emphasis added). If you knew someone planned to harm you, wouldn't you stay alert (1 Pet. 5:8)? The enemy's IQ outranks human intelligence. Thoughts and ideas that steal our joy, kill our hope, and destroy our faith and family originate with him—no matter who delivers them. Arrest them before they take root in your mind.

Satan Uses Deception

"There is no truth in him. . . . for he is a liar and the father of lies" (John 8:44).

"For Satan himself masquerades as an angel of light" (2 Cor. 11:14).

Satan disguises his schemes as brilliant ideas or the Holy Spirit's guidance. He may attach Scripture to his lies, like when he tempted Jesus (Matt. 4:5-6). He wraps evil in noble-sounding labels.

Satan Uses People

We know the devil uses unbelievers. But he also cons believers. Think of what we lost because Eve believed Satan's lies. Jesus spotted Satan behind Peter's plea to reject the cross.

> Peter took him aside and began to rebuke him. "Never, Lord!" he said. "This shall never happen to you!"
>
> Jesus turned and said to Peter, "Get behind me, Satan! You are a stumbling block to me; you do not have in mind the concerns of God, but merely human concerns." (Matt. 16:22-23)

Ananias and Sapphira, inspired by the devil, lied about a gift they'd given to the church (Acts 5:3–5). Their deception cost them their lives. In contrast to our enemy, Jesus delivers life and peace.

Life-giving: "I have come that they may have life, and
   have it to the full" (John 10:10).
Truthful: "Jesus answered, 'I am the way, and the truth
   and the life'" (John 14:6).
Gentle: "I am gentle and humble in heart" (Matt. 11:29).
Gracious: "All spoke well of him and were amazed at the
   gracious words that came from his lips" (Luke 4:22).
Loving: "God is love. Whoever lives in love lives in God,
   and God in them" (1 John 4:16).

The Good Shepherd doesn't accuse, taunt, shame, or generate irrational fears. If you hear a harsh tone when you read the Bible, where is it coming from? While Jesus dealt strongly with the religious hypocrites, which he likened to thieves, robbers, wolves, and hired hands (John 10), he gently leads his sheep and carries his lambs (Isa. 40:11).

Satan doesn't hold a gun to our heads. He wields lies, fear, envy, pride, bitterness, and disappointment. He touches our wounds to beat us into submission. If we succumb, he turns from tempter to accuser and shames us for falling for his tricks. Let's look at how Satan manipulated believers into doing his work and learn from their falls.

Scripture Reading..
EVE: GENESIS 1:27–30; 2:16–17; 3:1–8
DAVID: 1 CHRONICLES 21:1–8
US: 2 CORINTHIANS 10:3–5

Study and Reflection

1. The devil wanted to steal Adam and Eve's right to rule over creation (Gen. 1:27–30; 2:16–17). How did he get Eve to doubt God's character and disobey his one restriction (Gen. 3:1–8)?

2. Satan incited King David, who'd begun by trusting in the name of the Lord, to take a census and glory in the size of his army (1 Chron. 21:1–8). David didn't recognize Satan's influence. What warning do you draw from this?

3. "Dear friends, do not believe every spirit, but test the spirits to see whether they are from God . . . . You, dear children, are from God and have overcome them, because the one who is in you [Holy Spirit] is greater than the one who is in the world [the devil]" (1 John 4:1, 4). The better we know Jesus and live according to his Word, the easier it is to discern truth from falsehood. Contrast the spirit that comes from the world with what God gives. "For God has not given us a spirit of fear and timidity, but of power, love, and self-discipline" (2 Tim. 1:7 NLT).

4. How can practicing the following wisdom protect us from falling like Eve and David?

   a. "Do not love this world nor the things it offers you, for when you love the world, you do not have the love of the Father in you. For the world offers only a craving for physical pleasure, a craving for everything we see, and pride in our achievements and possessions. These are not from the Father but are from this world" (1 John 2:15–16 NLT).

   b. "But if you harbor bitter envy and selfish ambition in your hearts, do not boast about it or deny the truth. Such 'wisdom' does not come down from heaven but is earthly, unspiritual, demonic" (James 3:14–15).

5. Considering what you've read today, how do you apply 2 Corinthians 10:3–5?

6. Record your final thoughts from today's lesson.

Don't Be Deceived

Satan gaped. How could God create Adam and Eve in his image and give them the ability and authority to rule over creation? How dare God give humans what Satan surely deserved. Satan couldn't steal these gifts against the humans' will. Could he trick them? Would someone with perfect health, a home in paradise, and an ideal marriage listen to him? Maybe he could get them to question God's character. Nothing obvious. "Did God really say . . . ?"

Eve's response heartened him. She wasn't sure exactly what God had said. The serpent slithered through this crack. Pride had been his downfall. He appealed to Eve's. "God knows that when you eat from it your eyes will be opened, and you'll be like God" (Gen. 3:5).

Have you ever blamed your sins on your circumstances? "I didn't sleep well; I'm under a deadline." Perfect conditions didn't keep Eve from questioning the Lord's goodness. Was he holding out on her? She swallowed Satan's lie, "You rule over God's creatures. Surely, you know what's best for yourself?"

When you doubt Jesus cares about your needs and concerns, remember he left his throne in heaven, put on human flesh, and died to restore what Satan stole from you. Jesus is not the thief.

The following acronym—DARTS—can help you distinguish between the devil and our deliverer.

DARTS are:	Jesus is our:
Destructive: sent to steal, kill, and destroy (John 10:10). They push us away from God's perfect will and cause us to question our God-given desires or reservations. *You'll offend your neighbor if you invite her to Bible study.*	**Deliverer:** Jesus's words bring life and peace.
Accusing: condemning. These thoughts may begin with "if," as when Satan tempted Jesus. "If you are the Son of God . . ." Satan misused Scripture with Jesus, and he twists verses with us (Matt. 4:1–11). When Scripture oppresses you or causes you to doubt your standing with God, recognize your enemy. *If you were a good Christian . . .*	**Advocate:** While the Holy Spirit points out sin, Jesus never guilts, shames, or condemns us (Matt. 11:29; Rom. 8:1).
Rule-oriented: relying on standards for righteousness instead of on Christ's righteousness. They focus on following rules to prove ourselves. If we don't obey these human rules, our thoughts punish us. *Good Christians are self-sacrificing. How can I say no to this need?*	**Righteousness:** Jesus reminds us that our righteousness is found in Christ alone, not in our performance (Phil. 3:9; Col. 2:20–23).
Tempting: offering ways to meet our needs apart from God. *People will respect you if . . . . Hurry or you'll miss out.*	**Tower of strength:** Jesus infuses us with courage to stand alone, to be still and know, to please him even if it means disappointing people.
Slanderous: maligning the character of God, other people, or yourself. *God doesn't care about you.* Or, *Your friend is so selfish.*	**Shield:** Jesus reminds us he is with us and for us (Heb. 13:5; Rom. 8:31–34). His Spirit empowers us with love and patience (Gal. 5:22–23).

Today's Strength Builder

Practice distinguishing your shepherd's voice from imitations.

CLOSING PRAYER

Use this space to turn your insights and responses into prayers.

Day Three

Strong Armor for Weak Warriors

"It is not by sword or spear that the LORD saves;
for the battle is the LORD's."
—1 Samuel 17:47

Anyone who's ever tried to substitute a Phillips screwdriver for a flathead knows the importance of the right tool. The same applies to armor. Sunscreen protects from sunburn but not from frostbite. Shoulder pads won't shield a soccer player's shins. The right protection makes the difference.

God tells us to be strong in the Lord and in the strength of his might. His armor covers weak warriors with supernatural protection so they can fearlessly face towering giants.

Guard Your Borders

Did you know bamboo won the Guinness World Record for the fastest growing plant in the world?[3] We hardly noticed our neighbor's bamboo had migrated into our yard until tall stalks popped up overnight beside our house. My daughter spent days cutting back the intruding jungle only to have two stalks replace every one she removed.

One landscaper suggested backhoeing our yard and pouring a cement trench. Another suggested we move. To prevent a bamboo invasion, you need an underground barrier.

Like bamboo, half-truths send runners that sprout and choke our thoughts and emotions. It's easier to block their entrance than to beat back negative attitudes that have become deeply rooted.

What weed has invaded your mind's garden? Weeds pop up as fears, regrets, personal weaknesses, and false ideologies at church, the workplace, or your child's school. Battles that attack our faith and relationships have a spiritual component. If we don't understand this, we'll use the wrong weapons. God has provided the armor you need to win your battle.

Scripture Reading..
EPHESIANS 6:10–15
JAMES 4:6–7

Study and Reflection

1. Remember David's words? "It is not by sword or spear that the LORD saves; for the battle is the LORD's" (1 Sam. 17:47). From Ephesians 6:10, describe God's power.

2. Our enemy draws our focus onto the wrong agent. Who is our real enemy, and why is human strength inadequate to beat this foe (Eph. 6:11–13)?

3. The Bible describes our threefold enemy as the world, the flesh, and the devil. Renewing our minds (Rom. 12:2) and avoiding temptations (Matt. 6:13; 2 Tim. 2:22) protect us from the world and the flesh. How do we face spiritual warfare (Eph. 6:10–15; James 4:6–7)?

4. Record your final thoughts from today's lesson.

Be Careful

"So, if you think you are standing firm, be careful that you don't fall!"
—1 Corinthians 10:12

Remember Alexander the Great? The mighty conqueror that subdued kingdoms died from a fever that probably came from a mosquito bite. Don't ignore the small things.

When the promise of satisfaction lies just outside of God's will, remember Eve, and recognize the one lurking behind the temptation. Any satisfaction that requires disobedience will be short-lived at best. Eve didn't become like God. She fell like Satan, was ousted from her throne, and was marred by her fall. Her body began its slow march toward death. She must have wondered how she could have ever wanted the knowledge of evil when her firstborn murdered his younger brother. Her loss became our loss. Sin's consequences can't be contained.

Perhaps the loss of youthful vigor made David, a man after God's own heart, susceptible to Satan's idea to count Israel's armies. His sin cost seventy thousand men their lives. We need strength beyond ourselves to recognize and stand against the devil. And we have it.

I also pray that you will understand the incredible greatness of God's power for us who believe him. This is the same mighty power that raised Christ from the dead and seated him in the place of honor at God's right hand in the heavenly realms. Now he is far above any ruler or authority or power or leader or anything else— not only in this world but also in the world to come. (Eph. 1:19–21 NLT)

Today's Strength Builder

Practice guarding your thoughts. Which ones need to be captured and made to bow before Jesus?

CLOSING PRAYER

Use this space to turn your insights and responses into prayers.

Day Four
Buckle Up with Truth

In J. R. R. Tolkien's *The Lord of the Rings,* even wise Gandalf couldn't believe Frodo, a small hobbit, could survive a wound from the dreaded Ringwraiths. The mystery clears when he spies Frodo's mithril undergarment. When we clothe ourselves in the Lord's armor, the devil shudders. Like Frodo's mithril shirt, the invisible armor of God provides supernatural protection without weighing us down.

Satan punches us with lies. He manipulated Eve with words. Maybe that's why Paul begins with the belt of truth.

Scripture Reading..

EPHESIANS 6:13–14

1 JOHN 3:18–24

Study and Reflection

1. Belt of truth: Whether we need to break free from an emotional whirlwind or storm hell's gates to rescue a loved one, truth defeats "the father of lies" (John 8:32, 44). Claiming the truth of God's character and our Christian identity clears the emotional smog so we can see clearly. It's not enough to know correct doctrine (James 2:19); we must practice it (2 John 1:4).

    Declare the following truths and notice if any doubts arise. Look up the scripture associated with those that need reinforcing. Feel free to add others. God—

    -   Loves me (Jer. 31:3; John 3:16)
    -   Values me (Matt. 6:26)
    -   Guides me (Ps. 23:3, 73:24)
    -   Provides for me (Ps. 23:1; Matt. 6:25–33)
    -   Didn't make a mistake creating me (Ps. 139:13–14; Eph. 1:4, 2:10)
    -   Has given me everything I need to live a godly and satisfying life (2 Pet. 1:3)
    -   Is bigger than my mistakes (Rom. 8:28)
    -   Will never leave me (Matt. 28:20; Heb. 13:5)
    -   Has planned a good future for me (Jer. 29:11; Ps. 23:6)
    -   Other:

2. What thoughts tempt, accuse, condemn, or hinder your closeness with the Lord? What thoughts argue against your knowledge of God (2 Cor. 10:3–5)? Ask God to expose the lie behind your struggle.

3. The breastplate of righteousness: "Our righteous acts are like filthy rags" and provide no protection against the enemy (Isa. 64:6). But we have Christ's spotless righteousness (2 Cor. 5:21). God provides this righteousness the moment we invite Jesus to forgive our sins and be our Lord and Savior. We aren't saved by our works, but we are saved to do good works (Eph. 2:8–18, 5:8–10). Righteous living protects us from evil. Condoning sin is like Frodo removing his mithril shirt and marching into the enemy's camp waving a red flag. Read Galatians 5:19–23 and ask God to reveal any area where you've opened the door to demonic influences (such as pride, gossip, bitterness, dishonesty, comparison, immoral relationships, dabbling in the occult, or anti-Christian music and entertainment). By faith, renounce and forsake those areas now.

4. Record your final thoughts from today's lesson.

In the Clutches of Fear

No use trying to sleep. My husband Larry was traveling. It was up to me to keep watch—or so I felt. I sat in my favorite chair and wondered, *What's wrong with me? Why am I so afraid?*

My first flashes of fear started after becoming engaged to Larry. One day, out of nowhere, scenes of head-on collisions exploded in my mind while zigzagging along Colorado's majestic Big Thompson Canyon. The message was clear: Life is fragile. Happiness could end in an instant.

The fears resurfaced with our daughter's birth. Her beautiful face and tiny fingers awakened a plethora of emotions—including a fierce sense of protection.

Motherhood arrived with a radar for tragic stories about children. When the news reported a child died after walking too near a tiger's cage, I promised to never let my child near a wild animal cage.

My anxiety might have died except for some bizarre events. The trouble began on my birthday.

My friend Linda popped over to cook supper since Larry was out of town. While we savored chopped steak smothered with grilled mushrooms and onions, the phone rang. I grabbed it, hoping it was Larry. This was before caller ID. A male voice asked for Larry.

"He's not available," I said.

"I wanted to talk to you." The caller then asked me to lunch. I stammered a decline.

"You sounded like you were getting out of a date," Linda said.

"I was."

When Larry phoned, I told him about the call, hoping he'd say the man was a harmless neighbor. But Larry didn't know him. He wanted our friend Chris to call the stranger back to find out what was going on. What Chris learned amplified my concerns.

The name the caller gave belonged to the deceased husband of the widow across the street. That meant the caller knew where I lived.

I called the local police. The officer who took my call said, "Lady, it's not a crime to use a dead man's name."

"But I'm married, and he asked me out."

"It's not a crime to ask you out." Then he softened. "If it makes you feel better, we'll send a patrol car down your street."

Having a police car drive down my street once didn't reassure me. Thank you very much! Linda and I grabbed my eight-month-old daughter and left for her place.

I almost forgot about the incident until a crumpled note saying "Call John" appeared on my front door. The number went to a business where no John worked.

At 3 a.m. another night, frantic pounding on our front door sent my heart racing. This time Larry was home. A woman who looked like a medium seeking a séance apologized, "Ohh, wrong house."

The night my fears came to a head, Larry was away again. Our local news urgently warned that a serial killer who targeted women my age was loose. He entered through open windows. Our sixty-year-old arts and crafts bungalow didn't have air conditioning.

Did I have to choose between suffocation and strangulation?

I planned escape routes. But I couldn't figure out how to get my baby and me out in seconds. Exhausted but too afraid to sleep, I prayed. "Lord, please, deliver me from this fear." As an afterthought, I added, "Why am I so afraid?"

I immediately sensed his answer, "You don't think I care enough or am strong enough to protect you."

Was this true? I taught young women to trust God. Could this be about my relationship with God—not my circumstances?

I lost my mother to cancer when I was a teenager. If God loved me and was able to stop harm, why hadn't he spared her life? If he had allowed tragedy once, could I trust him now? Did God love me? Was he able to protect me? If I was going to fully trust God, I needed answers.

Does God love me?

In answer, I remembered Jesus on the cross. I recalled his anguish the night before his crucifixion. Jesus didn't want to go to the cross, but he endured that agony for me. "Greater love has no one than this: to lay down one's life for one's friends" (John 15:13). The cross irrevocably proved the depth of God's love.

I turned to my other question. Was God able to protect me?

Genesis chapter 1 says God spoke, and *bam*, what he said happened. That's power! Christ's resurrection alone proves God's power. There could be no doubt. God was able to protect me.

If God loved me and was able to protect me, why hadn't he shielded our family?

The intense protection I felt for my daughter had taught me something about parental love. I realized that just as my baby couldn't understand why I allowed her doctor to prick her with needles, I couldn't understand God's ways. I would do anything to protect her, and God's love is purer than mine. The pain God allows his children must serve a greater purpose.

Joseph told his brothers who had sold him into slavery, "You intended to harm me, but God intended it for good to accomplish what is now being done, the saving of many lives" (Gen. 50:20). God never said all things would be good, but he promised to work all things together for the good of those who love him (Rom. 8:28).

The evidence said God loved me and was able to care for me. Now I had to decide—would I trust him?

I knelt and prayed, "Lord, I choose to trust you. If you allow the worst I can imagine, I will trust that it is because you have something better than I can envision. I trust you to be with me through whatever you allow."

Relief washed over me. That night I slept like my baby.

Ironically, the incidents stopped. God used those disturbances to uncover and address my buried doubts. I can't say I've never felt afraid since, but when fear creeps in, I return to God's character. I can't imagine Jesus to be more loving or more powerful than he is.

Are you struggling with a recurring fear, doubt, or other paralyzing emotion? Ask God to uncover the lies you've swallowed. Then belt yourself in truth.

When we arrive in heaven and see our life's story from God's viewpoint, we won't shake our fists and say, "I knew you messed up with my life." We will raise our hands in praise. Since we won't be disappointed when we see clearly, let's rest in what we don't understand now.

Today's Strength Builder

Ask God to reveal any hidden stronghold that hinders your walk of faith.

CLOSING PRAYER

Use this space to turn your insights and responses into prayers.

Armor Up—the Days Are Evil

"All God's giants have been weak men who did great things for God because they reckoned on his being with them."
—J. Hudson Taylor[4]

The Bible says God works all things together "for the good of those who love him" (Rom. 8:28). However, this isn't always obvious. Faith must fill the gap between hoping and seeing.

First-century Rabbi Akiva (or Akiba) demonstrated his faith by habitually saying, "All the Merciful One does, he does for good."[5] The following story illustrates his practice.

Traveling at dusk, Akiva entered a village seeking shelter for the night. Door after door turned him away. "This, too, is for the best," Akiva said and led his donkey into the nearby woods.

After Akiva settled down, the wind picked up and blew out his candle. In the darkness someone or something snatched his rooster and donkey. Akiva said, "All the Merciful One does is for good."[6]

During the night, Romans pillaged the nearby village and captured the inhabitants. If not for God's providence, the soldiers would have seen his candle or heard his animals and captured him too. God had worked for Akiva's very best.[7]

By faith, Avika trusted God in the moment. Later God allowed him to see how he had worked rejection and loss together for Avika's good. A weaker saint would have given into self-pity or bitterness. Avika avoided this pit by practicing his faith during his disappointments.

The apostle John wrote, "I am writing to you, young men, because you have overcome the evil one" (1 John 2:13). How do we overcome the evil one? By facing our battles in faith. No one ever learned to swim by sitting on the sidelines. Let's suit up—because the days are evil (Eph. 5:16).

Scripture Reading..

EPHESIANS 6:15–20

"Therefore, since we have been made right in God's sight by faith, we have peace with God because of what Jesus Christ our Lord has done for us." —Romans 5:1 (NLT)

Study and Reflection

1. Shod in the gospel of peace: Cleats keep athletes from slipping. We can't confidently resist the devil if we doubt our standing with God or base it on anything other than the gospel (Rom. 5:1). Uncertainty over our relationship with God causes stumbles. Are you at peace with God? On what foundation are you building your relationship with him? What causes you to doubt your standing with God?

2. The shield of faith: The enemy personalizes the flaming arrows he releases on you. Suppose the "You're unlovable" arrow pierces your heart. God's Word says God has loved you with an everlasting love (Jer. 31:3). Or Satan whispers, "Trouble's coming." But Jesus says, "Fear not" (Isa. 41:10), and, "Do not worry about tomorrow" (Matt. 6:34). Whose message will you believe? The longer Satan's arrows burn, the longer we suffer. Ask God to reveal any arrows scorching you. Extinguish them with the shield of faith. (You can review Day Four, question 2.) Record your experience.

3. The helmet of salvation: One night, a high school football game tackle knocked my son unconscious and left him briefly disoriented. Thankfully, his helmet protected him from serious trauma, and he quickly recovered. Life tackles believers too. The helmet of salvation protects our minds when we get knocked around (1 Cor. 2:16). According to the following, why is it important to govern our thoughts? "The mind governed by the flesh is death, but the mind governed

by the Spirit is life and peace. The mind governed by the flesh is hostile to God; it does not submit to God's law, nor can it do so" (Rom. 8:6–7).

4. The sword of the Spirit: Linda Evans Shepherd says, "The sword of the Spirit is God's Word ignited with the power of God's Spirit."[8] The Greek word translated "word" in Ephesians 6:17 is *rhema*. The emphasis is on speaking the Word. In battle, we declare the scriptures in the power of the Holy Spirit. When Satan tempted Jesus, he quoted the Old Testament (Matt. 4:1–11). Practice speaking God's truth this week. Trust the Spirit to use the scriptures you quote to give you victory. For example, based on Psalm 23, we might say, "Because the Lord is my shepherd, I have everything I need." What scriptures help you slash the enemy's lies?

5. Record your final thoughts from today's lesson.

Who's Your Daddy? Or How to Be Assured of Your Salvation

David stood before King Saul holding Goliath's head. "Whose son are you?" Saul asked David. *And why are you carrying that disgusting head?*

King Saul failed to realize David's remarkable courage came from his heavenly Father, not his earthly one. Our actions reflect on our heavenly Father too.

Do you live with the assurance that God is with you? Can a person be assured they're forgiven, belong to God, and are going to heaven? Or do we live the best we can and hope we won't be disappointed?

When I was in college, a young woman involved in a campus ministry asked me when I'd become a Christian. I told her I'd grown up in the church and walked forward to ask Christ into my heart at every revival.

"You only have to ask Jesus into your heart once," she said. "When you ask in faith, he comes to permanently dwell in you."

That was news to me. I thought to make up for the inconsistencies in my life, I had to keep asking Jesus into my heart. That afternoon, Sharon explained how to gain assurance of my salvation. In case you or someone you love struggles with this, let's look at three reasons why a believer may doubt their salvation and three biblical assurances.

Three Reasons People Doubt Their Salvation

1. An unclear spiritual birthday. Just as everyone has a physical birthday, believers have a spiritual birthday. At salvation, we are born again (John 3:3). We move from darkness into light (Eph. 5:8), from death into life (Col. 2:13), and from being God's enemy to being his beloved child (Rom. 5:10; John 1:12). For some, especially those raised in the church, pinpointing a specific spiritual birthday may be difficult.

I had many aha moments when my heart thrilled at the reality of God. It took some reflection to identify the time I understood my need for the Savior. I remembered my heart being broken at church camp when I realized Jesus had died for *my* sins. I believe that is when I joined God's family (John 1:12). I returned home bursting with joy.

Charles Ryrie said, "People are either saved or lost at any given moment. No one grows into conversion. But we all do grow in our comprehension of conversion. So, although in God's sight and in our experience there was a point in time when we were saved, in our recollection or understanding we may not be able to specify it."[9]

2. Doubts over the procedure. Some people struggle with assurance because they aren't sure they did it right. If their conversion was private, they worry they didn't publicly walk an aisle. They focus on the process instead of on the promise.

"But to all who believed him and accepted him, he gave the right to become children of God" (John 1:12 NLT).

3. An ongoing struggle with sin. Habitual sin causes some people to question their salvation. Because "we all stumble in many ways" (James 3:2), it's vital to remember salvation is based on God's grace—not human performance. Those who willfully continue in sin without regret have reason to be concerned. Sin grieves the indwelling Holy Spirit, and godly sorrow leads to repentance—or change. Understanding the transformation that occurred when we were born into God's family (2 Cor. 5:17) and the ministry of the Holy Spirit provides victory over sin (Gal. 5:16). "The godly may trip seven times, but they will get up again" (Prov. 24:16 NLT).

Three Scriptural Assurances

1. We can enjoy a higher quality of life now and spend eternity with Jesus in heaven. "For God so loved the world that he gave his one and only Son, that whoever believes in him shall not perish but have eternal life" (John 3:16).

2. We can resolve our doubts. Eternal security rests on one question. What have I done with Jesus? "Whoever has the Son has life; whoever does not have the Son of God does not have life. I write these things to you who believe in the name of the Son of God so that you may know that you have eternal life" (1 John 5:12–13).

If, by faith, you've invited Jesus to be your Savior, then you have eternal life. Jesus never turns anyone away who comes to him in faith (John 6:37). Our faith rests in God's promises not our performance (John 1:12; Rev. 3:20).

3. We must live by faith. You didn't earn salvation, so you can't un-earn it. "God saved you by his grace when you believed. And you can't take credit for this; it is a gift from God. Salvation is not a reward for the good things we have done, so none of us can boast about it." (Eph. 2:8–9 NLT). God adopts us into his forever family and gives us a new nature like his (Eph. 4:24). He completes the work he began in us (Phil. 1:6).

Salvation boils down to faith. If you aren't sure you belong to God, you can make sure now. God wants his children to be secure in his love. You can express your faith through a simple prayer like this:

> *Lord Jesus, I confess I have sinned and fallen short of your glory. Thank you for dying on the cross for my sins. Come into my life and make me the person you created me to be.*

You need only ask Jesus into your life one time. Ask in faith. Move from doubt to thanksgiving. He's promised to never leave you or forsake you. Write the date in your Bible. If doubts surface, thank God he heard you the first time and reaffirm your desire to honor him with your life. Now go forth with confidence as God's beloved child and connect with other believers who walk with Jesus. We were never meant to take this spiritual journey alone (Heb. 10:25; 1 Pet. 2:4–5).

Today's Strength Builder

If you struggle with assurance of salvation, settle that doubt today. If you're not a part of a group of grace-filled, Bible-believing

Christians, ask God to provide one for you. Then ask around for one or start one (Matt. 18:20).

CLOSING PRAYER
Use this space to turn your insights and responses into prayers.

Prayer Requests

Afterword

Stronger than Death

"There were others who were tortured, refusing to be released so that they might gain an even better resurrection."
—Hebrews 11:35

In 1956, the murder of five American missionaries in Ecuador stunned the Christian world. These men and their families sought to carry the gospel to a people known for killing each other as easily as they killed their enemies. "Their initial friendly contact ended in death by spearing."[1]

Nate Saint, Jim Elliot, Roger Youderian, Ed McCully, and Peter Fleming spent their lives training for this mission. Why would God let their outreach end in tragedy? Why allow five young women to be widowed and nine children to be left fatherless?

Their killers heard singing and saw what could only have been angels in the trees surrounding the bodies. The Huaorani recognized the supernatural nature of what they witnessed.

If God is good, how do we reconcile the killing of these men? How do we understand the untimely death of our loved ones?

Steve Saint, whose father Nate was among the slain, wrote,

God took five common young men of uncommon commitment and used them for his own glory. They never had the privilege they so enthusiastically pursued

to tell the Huaorani of the God they loved and served.
But for every Huaorani who today follows God's trail . . .
there are a thousand cowodi [outsiders] who follow
God's trail more resolutely because of their example.
This success withheld from them in life God multiplied
and continues to multiply as a memorial to their
obedience and his faithfulness.[2]

Instead of crushing Christianity, the death of these missionaries ignited the spread of the gospel and spurred many to become missionaries. The tribe they wanted to reach eventually embraced Christ and took the message to others. Their deaths advanced the answer to their prayers in a way far greater than they could have imagined.

Death is not the end for the believer (Heb. 2:14). At the funeral of my friend's young adult son, the pastor said, "If it's not good, it's not over." The last words of another friend's husband echoed this hope: "Wow, wow, wow. It's all true! All of it. All the love, incredible."

A Better Resurrection

While we mourn the loss of our loved ones, believers don't mourn as the world mourns. Our grief is softened by hope. This was brought back to me recently.

On Good Friday, my phone rang. I didn't answer the unknown number. Later I checked my voicemail, and the voice of a dear friend asked how my dogs' haircuts turned out. The message jolted me. While both of my dogs had been groomed the day before, this friend had moved to heaven exactly six months earlier.

I don't know how an old message that dealt with a current event played when I hit voicemail. I do know I felt both sadness and joy. I miss Susie. During her cancer battle, I told her I was writing this book for her. She didn't live to see it finished. She received something better. Today, Susie lives in heaven, where she'll never suffer weakness or loss again.

Hebrews chapter 11 ends with a mystery: "For God had something better in mind for us, so that they would not reach perfection without us" (Heb. 11:40 NLT). Each of us is connected to every saint who has gone before us and to those who will come after us. Our individual stories are paragraphs woven into his grand story. Only when the last page is written will we completely understand the significance of our role in the great story of Christ Jesus. Only then will the dips in God's story make sense. Then faith will give way to sight.

I close with Jonathan Cahn's words: "Revelation closes with . . . 'and they shall reign forever and ever.' You see, the purposes of God have only perfect endings. And so for those who let him write their story, the ending is the same . . . perfect. Their ending . . . is heaven."[3]

Thank You

Thank you for reading *Little Strength, Big God*. I hope these stories and lessons continue to feed your faith. Please consider telling a friend and leaving an online review at your favorite bookseller. Your comments help others. For resources to refresh your faith or to keep in touch, go to RefreshingFaith.com. For more resources on this and other *Big God* books, go to debbiewwilson.com/book. God bless you.

Acknowledgments

I have been blessed with two special groups of women who meet weekly for Bible study. Their love for the Lord and for learning inspire me. Thank you, Jesus Girls, for letting me write for you. Your discussions polished my thoughts and helped shape this book. I must highlight some of you by name for your extra help: Susan Alexander, Sandi Brown, Amy Edwards, Tara Furman, Lisa Grimes, Kelly Hollis, Nan Sawaia, Dottie Stam, and Denita Thomas, you went far beyond the call of duty. You all enrich my life.

Thank you, Jason Fikes, Mary Hardegree, Duane Anderson, and the Leafwood team, for your feedback and work to publish and release *Little Strength, Big God*. I'm grateful for the privilege of working with you on three Big God books now.

A special shoutout to Stephen Mathisen and PeggySue Wells for your contributions. And finally, my heartfelt appreciation to my family, Larry Wilson, Ginny Wilson, and Brant Wilson, for your support and encouragement. May our efforts bring glory to our Big God.

Other Books by Debbie

Little Faith, Big God
ISBN: 978-1-68426-430-8

Little Women, Big God
ISBN: 978-0-89112-386-6

Give Yourself a Break
ISBN: 978-1-50871-931-1

Social Media

https://www.pinterest.com/djwwilson/
Twitter: @debbieWwilson
https://www.instagram.com/debbieWwilson/
https://www.facebook.com/debbieWwilsonauthor/

Notes

WEEK ONE

[1] Adapted from https://truthbook.com/stories/funny-stories/funny-animals/german-shepherd-doberman-cat/, accessed December 22, 2022.

[2] Mei Fong, "Sterilization, Abortion, Fines: How China Brutally Enforced Its 1-Child Policy," *New York Post*, January 3, 2016, http://nypost.com/2016/01/03/how-chinas-pregnancy-police-brutally-enforced-the-one-child-policy/.

[3] John MacArthur, *The MacArthur New Testament Commentary: Hebrews* (Chicago: Moody Bible Institute, 1983), 345.

[4] "World Watch List 2023: The Top 50 Countries Where It's Most Difficult to Follow Jesus," Open Doors, https://www.opendoorsus.org/en-US/persecution/countries/.

[5] Anne Graham Lotz, "Paying the Ultimate Price," *Hugh's News* blog, October 11, 2017, https://www.hughsnews.com/newsletter-posts/paying-the-ultimate-price-by-anne-graham-lotz.

[6] Blue Letter Bible, "Dictionaries :: Jochebed," *International Standard Bible Encyclopaedia*, https://www.blueletterbible.org/search/Dictionary/viewTopic.cfm?topic=IT0005080.

[7] Bruce W. Martin, *Desperate for Hope: Hanging on and Finding God during Life's Hardest Times* (Grand Rapids: Revell, 2012), 208–9.

[8] Candyce Carden, "Military Mom: Learning to Trust God," *Candyce Carden* blog, accessed December 29, 2022, https://candycecarden.com/military-mom-learning-to-trust-god/.

[9] Beverly McMillan, "I Was an Abortionist. What I Saw Turned Me into a Lifelong Pro-Life Activist," DailyWire, accessed December 22, 2022, https://www.dailywire.com/news/i-was-an-abortionist-what-i-saw-turned-me-into-a-lifelong-pro-life-activist.

[10] "Healing the Hurt of a Past Abortion," *Focus on the Family*, October 31, 2022, https://www.focusonthefamily.com/pro-life/abortion/healing-the-hurt-of-a-past-abortion/.

WEEK TWO

[1] Blue Letter Bible, "Lexicon :: Strong's H4872 – *mōšê*," *Strong's Concordance*, https://www.blueletterbible.org/lexicon/h4872/kjv/wlc/0-1/.

[2] Jonathan Cahn, *The Book of Mysteries* (Lake Mary, FL: Charisma House Book Group, 2018), 231.

[3] Susie's story is told with her permission.

[4] Bruce W. Martin, *Desperate for Hope* (Grand Rapids: Revell, 2012), 21.

[5] Vladislav Tchakarov, "10 Most Significant Treasures Found in Tutankhamun's Tomb in Pictures," *Curiosmos*, September 27, 2020, https://curiosmos.com/10-most-significant-treasures-found-in-tutankhamuns-tomb-in-pictures/.

[6] J. Vernon McGee, *Thru the Bible with J. Vernon McGee*, vol. 5 (Pasadena, CA: Thru the Bible Radio, 1983), 592

[7] Charles R. Swindoll, *Swindoll's Living Insights New Testament Commentary*, vol. 12: *Hebrews* (Carol Stream, IL: Tyndale House Publishers, 2017), 190.

[8] Cahn, *Book of Mysteries*, 239.

[9] Dan Heath and Chip Heath, *Made to Stick: Why Some Ideas Survive and Others Die* (New York: Random House, 2007), 111–13.

[10] C. S. Lewis, *George MacDonald* (1974, reprint; New York: Collier Books, 1986), xxvi.

[11] Cahn, *Book of Mysteries*, 247.

[12] Cahn, *Book of Mysteries*, 268.

[13] Cahn, *Book of Mysteries*, 268.

[14] Brad the Painter, "How Long to Wait Between Coats of Paint?" *Brad the Painter*, September 21, 2021, https://www.bradthepainter.com/how-long-to-wait-between-coats-of-paint/.

[15] Warren W. Wiersbe, *Run with the Winners: A Study of the Champions of Hebrews 11* (Wheaton: Tyndale House Publishers, 1985), 110.

[16] Wiersbe, *Run with the Winners*, 101.

[17] Wiersbe, *Run with the Winners*, 108.

[18] Wiersbe, *Run with the Winners*, 112.

WEEK THREE

[1] Blue Letter Bible, "Lexicon :: Strong's H1897 - *hāgâ*: Outline of Biblical Usage, I. A. iii.," https://www.blueletterbible.org/lexicon/h1897/nasb95/wlc/0-1/.

[2] Debbie W. Wilson dedicates a whole chapter to Rahab in *Little Women, Big God* (Abilene, TX: Leafwood Publishers, 2016).

[3] Blue Letter Bible, "Lexicon :: Strong's H6942 - *qāḏaš*," *Strong's Concordance*, https://www.blueletterbible.org/lexicon/h6942/nasb20/wlc/0-1/.

[4] C. S. Lewis, *The Silver Chair*, book 4 in The Chronicles of Narnia (1953, reprint; New York: Collier Books, 1970), 210.

[5] Blue Letter Bible, "Lexicon :: Strong's G3670 - *homologeō*," *Vine's Expositiory Dictionary*, https://www.blueletterbible.org/lexicon/g3670/nasb95/tr/0-1/.

[6] Cahn, *Book of Mysteries*, 174.

WEEK FOUR

[1] John F. Walvoord and Roy B. Zuck, *The Bible Knowledge Commentary: Old Testament* (Colorado Springs: David C. Cook, 1985), 391.

[2] Blue Letter Bible, "Lexicon :: Strong's H1168 - *ba'al*," *Strong's Concordance*, https://www.blueletterbible.org/lexicon/h1168/kjv/wlc/ss1/0-1.

[3] In the Old Testament, the Spirit of the Lord came upon people to equip them for specific tasks. Today, the Holy Spirit lives in every believer's heart. He equips us to live holy lives and to fulfill our individual callings. Unlike in the Old Testament, he'll never leave us or forsake us (Heb. 13:5).

[4] Samson is discussed in *Little Faith, Big God*.

[5] *The Quest Study Bible, New International Version* (Grand Rapids: Zondervan), 332.

[6] Cahn, *Book of Mysteries*, 172.

[7] Levi Lusko, *Through the Eyes of a Lion: Facing Impossible Pain, Finding Incredible Power* (Nashville: W Publishing Group, 2015), xxv.

WEEK FIVE

[1] Blue Letter Bible, "Lexicon :: Strong's H1301 - *bārāq*," *Strong's Concordance*, https://www.blueletterbible.org/lexicon/h1301/kjv/wlc/0-1/.

[2] H. E. Finley, "Gods and Goddesses, Pagan," in *Evangelical Dictionary of Biblical Theology* (Grand Rapids: Baker Book House, 1996), e-book, 302.

[3] Randy Alcorn, *If God Is Good: Why Do We Hurt?* (Colorado Springs: Multnomah Books, 2010), 4.

[4] Neil T. Anderson, *Victory over the Darkness: Realize the Power of Your Identity in Christ* (Bloomington, MN: Bethany House, 2013), 112.

[5] Tony Evans, *Victory in Spiritual Warfare*, https://www.goodreads.com/author/quotes/2411.Tony_Evans.

[6] Jim Rohn, *The Treasury of Quotes by Jim Rohn* (1994, reprint; Southlake, TX: Jim Rohn International, 2006), 110.

[7] Blue Letter Bible, "Lexicon :: Strong's H3278 - *yā'ēl*," *Strong's Concordance*, https://www.blueletterbible.org/lexicon/h3278/kjv/wlc/0-1/.

[8] J. Vernon McGee, *Thru the Bible with J. Vernon McGee*, vol. 2 (Pasadena, CA: Thru the Bible Radio, 1982), 59.

WEEK SIX

[1] Blue Letter Bible, "Lexicon :: Strong's H3316 - *yip̄tāḥ*," *Strong's Concordance*, https://www.blueletterbible.org/lexicon/h3316/kjv/wlc/0-1/.

[2] John Foxe, *Foxe's Christian Martyrs* (Uhrichsville, OH: Barbour Publishing, 2010), 74.

[3] Mary Fairchild, "William Tyndale Biography: English Bible Translator and Christian Martyr," Learn Religions, March 3, 2019, https://www.learnreligions.com/william-tyndale-biography-700000.

[4] Charles Caldwell Ryrie, *The Ryrie Study Bible* (Chicago: Moody Press, 1978), 385.

[5] John F. Walvoord and Roy B. Zuck, *The Bible Knowledge Commentary* (Wheaton, IL: Scripture Press Publications, 2002), 214, 341.

[6] R. K. Harrison, *Leviticus: An Introduction and Commentary*, vol. 3 (Downers Grove, IL: InterVarsity Press, 1980), 240.

[7] A. E. Cundall and L. Morris, *Judges and Ruth: An Introduction and Commentary*, vol. 7 (Downers Grove, IL: InterVarsity Press, 1968), 143.

[8] Harrison, Leviticus, 240.

[9] *Oxford Languages Dictionary*, s.v. "halo effect," accessed January 13, 2023, https://www.google.com/search?client=safari&rls=en&q=halo+effect+definition&ie=UTF-8&oe=UTF-8.

WEEK SEVEN

[1] Roland Peterson, *The Good Humor Book* (Santa Anna, CA: Vision House Publishers, 1976), 113.

[2] Larry Osborne, *Thriving in Babylon: Why Hope, Humility, and Wisdom Matter in a Godless Culture* (Colorado Springs: David C. Cook, 2015), 39.

[3] Erwin W. Lutzer, *The Church in Babylon: Heeding the Call to Be a Light in the Darkness* (Chicago: Moody Publishers, 2018), 81.

[4] "סִירָס çârîyç, saw-reece'; or סָרַס çâriç; from an unused root meaning to castrate; a eunuch; by implication, valet (especially of the female apartments), and thus, a minister of state:—chamberlain, eunuch, officer." Blue Letter Bible, "Lexicon :: Strong's H5631 - *sārîs*," *Strong's Concordance*, https://www.blueletterbible.org/lexicon/h5631/nasb95/wlc/0-1/.

[5] Victor Hugo, *Things Seen [Choses Vues]*, vol. 1 (Glasgow: George Routledge and Sons, 1887), 88.

WEEK EIGHT

[1] G. K. Chesterton, *Illustrated London News*, January 14, 1911, accessed January 17, 2023, https://www.chesterton.org/quotations/war-and-politics/.

[2] Francis Schaeffer, "How the Elites Manipulate the Media to Control Us," YouTube, episode 10 from *How Should We Then Live?*, accessed January 18, 2023, https://www.youtube.com/watch?v=jianKzB753M.

[3] "Fastest Growing Plant," Guinness World Records, accessed January 18, 2023, https://www.guinnessworldrecords.com/world-records/fastest-growing-plant.

[4] Wiersbe, *Run with the Winners*, 134.

[5] Nissan Mindel, "Nachum Ish Gamzu and Rabbi Akiba," Chabad.org, accessed January 18, 2023, http://www.chabad.org/library/article_cdo/aid/112045/jewish/Nahum-Ish-Gamzu-and-Rabbi-Akiba.

[6] Mindel, "Nachum Ish Gamzu and Rabbi Akiba."

[7] Yael Eckstein, "All for the Best," International Fellowship of Christians and Jews, December 13, 2021, http://www.ifcj.org/learn/holy-land-moments/daily-devotionals/all-for-the-best.html.

[8] Linda Evans Shepherd, *Winning Your Daily Spiritual Battles: Living Empowered by the Armor of God* (Grand Rapids: Revell, 2016), 115.

[9] Charles Caldwell Ryrie, *Basic Theology: A Popular Systematic Guide to Understanding Biblical Truth* (Chicago: Moody Press, 1999), 380.

Afterword

[1] Steve Saint, "Did They Have to Die?," *Christianity Today*, September 16, 1996, http://www.christianitytoday.com/ct/1996/september16/6ta020.html.

[2] Saint, "Did They Have to Die?"

[3] Cahn, *Book of Mysteries*, 286.

Little Women, BIG GOD

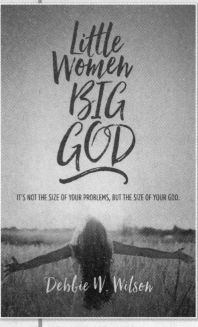

IT'S NOT THE SIZE OF YOUR PROBLEMS, BUT THE SIZE OF YOUR GOD.

Debbie W. Wilson

ISBN 978-0-89112-386-6

Meet the surprising women in Jesus's family tree as they journey through impossible circumstances and discover that quality of life is not determined by the size of our problems but by the size of our God. You will relate to Tamar, Rahab, Ruth, Bathsheba, and Mary as they face failure, loss, betrayal, and a murderous hunt. Discover God's care for ordinary women and how he uses human weakness and failure as an opportunity to reveal his strength and grace. Also, record God's faithfulness in your own journey of faith and see how everyday women who walk with Christ have meaningful stories worth telling. Finally, you'll learn faith in a Big God is life's only unshakable foundation.

"These pages helped me to realize the wonder and matchless love that a Big God has for this little woman. May all my days be spent boldly living out that love and truth."
    —**Amy Richissin,** development officer, Turning Point

"Today's challenges are not new to God. Using the stories of the women of old, Little Women, Big God shows you how to overcome your trials."
    —**DiAnn Mills,** author of *Deadlock* and *Deadly Encounter*

1-877-816-4455 toll free
www.leafwoodpublishers.com

LEAFWOOD
PUBLISHERS
an imprint of Abilene Christian University Press